SAINT ANDREW
Scotland's Myth and Identity

Michael T R B Turnbull

SAINT ANDREW PRESS

First published in 1997 by
SAINT ANDREW PRESS
121 George Street, Edinburgh EH2 4YN

Copyright © Michael T R B Turnbull 1997

ISBN 0 7152 0723 7

British Library Cataloguing in Publication Data
A catalogue record for this book
is available from the British Library.

ISBN 0715207237

Cover and **design concept** by Mark Blackadder.
Cover photograph by Paul Turner.
Typeset in 11/12 pt Bembo by Lesley A Taylor.
Printed and **bound** by Athenaeum Press Ltd, Gateshead, Tyne & Wear.

CONTENTS

MAP
Illustrating History of
THE CHURCH
During the Celtic Period.
Scale of Miles

NORTHERN PICTS

SOUTHERN PICTS

ANGLES OF
BERNICIA

BRETS OR STRATHCLUYDE

NIDUARI PICTS

Tracht Romin

CRUITHNIGH

DALRIADA

Northern Hy Neill

Cinel
Eoghain

Cinel
Conaill

i v

INTRODUCTION

A LEAP of the imagination is needed to unpick the ties between Scotland and St Andrew the Apostle. His story – and that of his bones – is essentially that of an explorer, a wanderer. The theme of his story is odyssey; his method of communication is networking.

It was not morbid curiosity nor pedantic interest that motivated those who came in quest of the earthly remains of Andrew the Apostle. Today speculation in this matter can be equally widespread and intense – as in the case of the search for the remains of Alexander the Great, Adolf Hitler, the Czar of Russia and his daughter Anastasia. Recent fears over the export of the St Thomas à Becket *chasse* (casket) – believed to have held the bones of the martyr – echo the importance which the bones of St Andrew held for Scots through most of their history.

The story of St Andrew grew with the story of Scotland. Andrew has been potently used as a rallying-point for countless Scots who left their native shores in the name of a cause, or who struggled to break new ground abroad – practical men and women who spent themselves in the search for ways of making the land and the elements work for them and the laws of physics and chemistry.

Like the other Apostles, Andrew's role was to communicate, persuade and then achieve. The function of saints has always been to motivate the living by their example. In her association with St Andrew, Scotland asserts a long-established European dimension, through links with Greece, Italy and the Ukraine. St Andrew symbolises Scotland's ruggedly individual characteristics and a unique integrity of aspiration and culture. To those who accept religion only as far as it exists in a rarefied vacuum of ethical purity and philosophical idealism, the story of St Andrew and Scotland gives the lie. Religious devotion, particularly in this case, is so tightly interwoven with warfare, politics, economics and sociology, as to be inseparable. In the final analysis, religion has as much a legitimate human view-point as it has a divine perspective. Religion is the inter-action of the two.

For Scots everywhere, St Andrew has always been a focus for nationhood. Through the ages he has been a unifying icon for forging Scotland's identity. This is his story …

MICHAEL T R B TURNBULL
August 1997

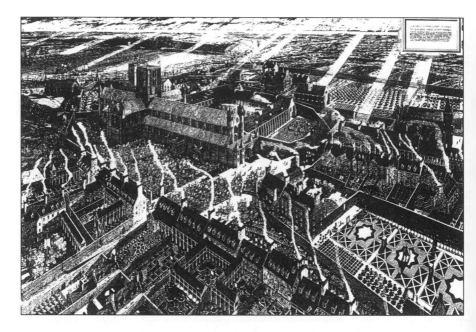

THE GLORIOUS HOUSE OF ST ANDREW, PALM SUNDAY 1540 –
GLORIOSA DOMUS SANCTI ANDREE
(BY JUREK PÜTTER DA)

ACKNOWLEDGMENTS

I AM very grateful for the advice and assistance
given to me by the following:

Revd John Weir Cook
Dr John Durkan
Dr Mark Dilworth OSB
Dr Christine Johnson
Professor Michael Lynch
Revd Glendon Macaulay
Dr John Purser
Jim Tracey
City of Edinburgh Libraries
Grafik Orzel Design Studio
Historic Scotland
The National Library of Scotland
The National Monument Record
New College Library
St Andrews Public Library
St Andrews University Library

DEDICATION

To
Celia, Sally
and the *Friends* of
Hawkhill Adult Training Centre

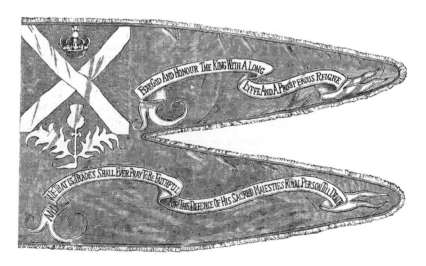

'THE BLUE BLANKET' –
STANDARD of the INCORPORATED TRADES of EDINBURGH

Chapter 1

ANDREW
IN THE
BIBLE

THE name *Andrew* in Greek means 'manly' or 'courageous'. Like many people of his day in Galilee, Andrew, as well as his native Aramaic, would probably have spoken some *koine* Greek, the *lingua franca* of the Roman Empire and the language in which the Gospels were evidently first written. This makes more plausible later accounts of Andrew's mission to preach and teach in Greece.

Although, along with the other Apostles, Andrew shared the daily life of Jesus, what we really know about Andrew is limited to a few tantalising glimpses. But, in all the other events of Jesus' ministry, Andrew can also be assumed to have participated with the other Apostles.

In the Gospels, Simon Peter and his brother Andrew (which was the younger, we are not told) first come to our notice on the shores of the Sea of Galilee. The Sea of Galilee – almost 210 metres below sea-level and shaped like a tear-drop – is some 20 kilometres long and varies between four and eleven kilometres wide. In depth the Sea of Galilee is around 45 metres and has been likened to a Scottish loch – the one it most resembles being the Lake of Mentieth. The Sea of Galilee was noted for fishing, boat-building and fish-curing.

Andrew and Peter, living in the principal port of Bethsaida (meaning 'Fisher Home'), are fisherman, sailing craft the size of small wooden whaling-boats, catching local fish (mainly a kind of mullet). Through long experience they would be skilled in reading the signs of clouds, winds and currents.

From Jerusalem, **Revd Colin Morton**, minister of St Andrew's Scots Memorial Church writes:

In 1986, at a time when the Sea of Galilee was low and some of the sea-bed uncovered, a first century AD fishing-boat was discovered buried in the mud. It was in a fair state, not complete, but sufficiently preserved so that experts could tell what it would have been like. It has been carefully preserved at Kibbutz Ginossar, kept in the dark and immersed in a wax solution for many years until the timber can withstand the atmosphere. The process has now been completed and the boat, which is called 'The Jesus Boat', is now open to view. Replicas have been produced and take pilgrims for trips on the lake so that they can experience what Jesus and his disciples did.

Fishing is an important industry as it was in Andrew's day. Twenty-two species of fish are still found in the lake. Even today fish can gather in great numbers where hot springs well up from the bed of the lake; indeed, the shoals of fish can often be seen better from a little height on the shore than they can from the boat on the surface, bringing the story in the twenty-first chapter of John's Gospel to mind. Still today sudden squalls can spring up, especially in the afternoon and people have to watch out for them.

There have been recent archaeological discoveries at Bethsaida, which was Andrew's home town as it was Peter's and Philip's [John 1:44]. There had been much mystery about Bethsaida, but now very clear remains of a fishing town have been uncovered a little distance from the present shore at the flat north-east corner of the lake. People surmise that the shore in New Testament times extended further inland.

In the Gospels we first see Andrew out of doors, hard at work. Matthew, in 4:18 of his Gospel, describes how Jesus was walking by the Sea of Galilee when he saw two fishermen: Simon, known as 'Peter', and his brother Andrew. Jesus, according to Matthew, witnesses the two men as they are casting their nets out into the lake and, like fishermen everywhere, one of Andrew's prime personal qualities appears to be perseverance.

Next we are told that Jesus begins to speak to them: (1) *'Follow me and I will make you fishers of men.'* Matthew records their reaction: (2) *'They left their nets and followed him.'* Whether they did so quickly, on impulse, or after mature consultation, is not made clear. All we are told is the names of the Apostles: (3) *'First, Simon who is called Peter, and his brother Andrew.'*

Mark (1:16) varies the account slightly. The two brothers are first seen by Jesus casting a net into the lake. Their reaction to Jesus' request to follow Him is that they leave their nets 'at once' – either a case of instantaneous conversion or spur-of-the-moment decision-making. But it was still an option that they would return to the fishing from time to time later on.

We next see Andrew (Mark 1:29) when Jesus is leaving the syna-gogue with James and John. All three arrive at the house of Simon and Andrew where Simon's mother-in-law is in bed with fever. The brothers immediately tell Jesus about her illness and Jesus goes to her and takes her by the hand. The fever subsides and Jesus helps her up. She starts to make them all welcome and to serve up some food.

In Mark (3:18) we are shown Jesus nominating twelve men to be his companions, among them Andrew. Their primary function is to be sent out to preach, with the power to cast out devils.

Much later in his ministry (in Mark 13:1-4), Jesus is seen in Jerusalem sitting on the slope of the Mount of Olives, looking at the Temple. Jesus has just told the disciples that the Temple will one day be destroyed.

In privacy, Peter, James, John and Andrew question him: (4) *'Tell us,'* they ask, *'when is this going to happen, and what sign will there be that all this is about to be fulfilled?'* And Jesus tells them of the coming destruction of Jerusalem and of his second coming on the Last Day, at the end of the world.

Luke (6:13) supplies the additional information that Jesus first called together his disciples and from them chose twelve as Apostles. Luke adds that they were called at dawn – (5) *'when day came'*.

From John (1:40) it emerges that Andrew was influenced into following Jesus by listening to the oratory of John the Baptist, the desert preacher. It was Andrew, John records (1:41-42), who then first introduced his brother Peter to Jesus. John states that it was around four o' clock in the afternoon when Andrew met his brother and told him that he had found the Messiah.

Andrew then takes Simon Peter to Jesus. Jesus looks hard at Peter and tells him: (6) *'You are Simon son of John; you are to be called* Cephas*'* – meaning 'Rock'.

John (1:44) adds that three of the Apostles – Philip, Andrew and Peter – all came from the town of Bethsaida.

Again it is Andrew (John 6:8), before the feeding of the five thousand, who takes the initiative and tells Jesus that there is a boy in the crowd who has five loaves of barley bread and two fish. Andrew, the practical fisherman, could see no way of making these slender provisions satisfy the needs of so many people.

Jesus and the disciples go to Jerusalem for Passover. By this time, Jesus had attracted considerable public interest through his raising of Lazarus from the dead. He and his followers had been welcomed to Jerusalem with hosannas and waving palms.

John (12:22) tells us that, among those who went up to worship at the festival, there were some who were not born Jewish but had been converted. They approached Philip and asked if they could meet Jesus. Philip goes to ask Andrew, and then Andrew takes Philip to Jesus.

In John, Andrew is presented as a personality who can be quoted, described and consulted in his own right. Andrew appears in a position of authority. He is placed in a position of leadership.

Our last glimpse of Andrew is in Acts (1:13). We are shown Andrew with Peter, John, James, Philip and Thomas, walking back from the Mount of Olives to the centre of Jerusalem after the crucifixion and death of their Master. When they reach the city they go to the upper room where they had previously been staying.

According to the New Testament accounts, Andrew was a man who took initiatives. He was the first Apostle, bringing his brother Peter to Christ. He also seems to have introduced Philip to Christ. And finally, in the case of the Jewish converts in Jerusalem, Andrew is the one who took it upon himself to be the first to bring those who were not Jews, to Christ. He was the first to bring Christ to the Gentiles.

This is the man our story is all about.

JESUS WITH HIS DISCIPLES

Chapter 2

ANDREW
IN LEGEND

THE information found in the Gospels relating to Andrew has a greater claim to authenticity than the often strange and curious exploits which fill the pages of the many later (but apocryphal) works which purport to be truthful accounts of his subsequent life.

If the New Testament gives only brief but significant glimpses of Andrew, many versions of the *Acts of Andrew* – and those of the other Apostles – flesh out the story of his mission to teach and preach, locating his mission-field in Greece and Asia Minor.

Over the centuries the subsequent labours of Andrew were piously (and sometimes heretically) worked up into a fantastic heroic tale, full of exaggerated details of miracles on the one hand, and of horrendous torment on the other; full of sermons delivered by the saint and apparent evidence of miracles worked by him.

These accounts are plainly attempts to turn Andrew into a folk-hero who embodied many of the spiritual characteristics of the countries and cultures for which the stories were written. They were designed to be vehicles of Christian teaching to the many cultures from which they sprang.

The convenient fact about Andrew is that only the bare bones of his life and character are known. This makes him a particularly suitable vehicle for imaginative theological transformation into a figure of superhuman exploits and extraordinary sufferings. The slender biographical details of Andrew's life form a fertile framework for the preacher or the travelling storyteller in the market-place or around the fire, to embroider out as necessary.

The later traditions record that Andrew preached in Greece, the Ukraine, Poland, and even in what is now Istanbul (Constantinople).

Andrew is said to have been tortured in the city of Patras in Greece and then left to die on a cross by the seashore. Traditionally the date of his death is celebrated as having been 30 November, a date Andrew shares with the Greek tragedian Euripides (died 406 BC) and the Anglo-Irish satirist Jonathan Swift (born 1667).

Most modern scholars regard these traditions as being at best impossible to verify, and at worst unhistorical. But even if these traditions are no more than the product of pious fancy anxious to catch the popular imagination, the extraordinary miracles and exploits of Andrew were to play an important part in the religious history of the Middle Ages.

Andrew's main claim to fame was to have been the *first* Apostle to be called by Jesus. He is mentioned in the apocryphal *Gospel of Peter* (*circa* AD 150) and later in the *Epistle of the Apostles* (*circa* AD 160) where Jesus asks Andrew to look at his feet and see if they made prints in the ground – the ghost of a devil being said to make no footprints on the earth.

Origen (*circa* AD 185-254), the Alexandrian scholar and teacher, writes that Andrew had a mission in Scythia. But even as early as the fourth century there were those, such as Bishop Philastrius of Brescia, who complained that the fables about Andrew and the other Apostles (in which they worked miracles where dogs and cattle were given human voices and souls) were wildly exaggerated and even heretical.

Later writers generally accepted the fact that Andrew was martyred in Greece around the year AD 70, but were sceptical as to the genuineness of his and other saints' mummified bodies and relics.

The many versions of the *Acts of Andrew* existed before the year AD 200, developing in four distinct but related cycles of stories – Egyptian, Byzantine, Latin and Syriac.

The exploits of Andrew, according to these texts, were colourful and awe-inspiring. First we are told that the Apostles drew lots as to where they were to preach Christianity. Andrew is said to have been told by Jesus in a vision that he must find a boat and sail to Sinope, the City of the Cannibals. As they set sail, Andrew and his companions found Jesus sitting at the rudder, piloting the ship. Some authorities locate this mission as taking place about the year AD 44.

Andrew is said to have driven out devils in Nicea and it is claimed that he also travelled to Thrace and Sevastopol. And in the town of Sinope, the aforementioned City of Cannibals, he found the inhabitants preparing to eat several human captives. Andrew prayed to God and the Devil appeared. The Devil encouraged the people to turn against Andrew. They tied a rope around Andrew's neck and dragged him through the streets, tearing off pieces of his body so that his blood flowed like water on the ground. Andrew escaped and afterwards fruit-trees grew on the spot where his blood had dropped.

Next Andrew continues his journey through Thessaly and Greece until he comes to Patras. There his conversion of the people angers the Roman proconsul Aegeates, especially when Andrew persuades the proconsul's wife, Maximilla, to reject the pagan gods.

Andrew is imprisoned by Aegeates. The proconsul has him scourged and crucified on the sand at the seashore. Andrew's hands and feet are not nailed, but *tied* to the cross. From the cross Andrew preaches to the great crowds around him until he dies.

Maximilla, the proconsul's wife, then takes Andrew's body down from the cross, washes and embalms it, and buries it on the seashore beside the prison. From that time Maximilla lives apart from her husband. Aegeates, however, is driven insane and eventually throws himself to his death from the roof of his official residence.

Such is the storyline, which varies in detail from one version to another. The long rambling sermons of Andrew, and the sadistic descriptions of his torments, are evidence of history out of control, of fact at the service of propaganda, however well-intentioned. The lurid and exaggerated details of the apocryphal *Acts of Andrew* are very different from the low-key, commonsense narrative of the Gospels.

Other writers allege more personal biographical details about Andrew. He is, for example, said to have been unmarried (unlike Peter, who had a wife and children). He was older than Peter, but was baptised by Peter.

Of what we know today as the 'Saint Andrew's Cross', there is no mention. Andrew, at most, is said to have been crucified upright (unlike his brother Peter, who was crucified upside-down). And Andrew is said to have been tied (not nailed) to a forked or Y-shaped olive-tree.

However, this was, around the tenth century, developed into the *decussate* (x-shaped cross) – insert – which additionally mirrors the Greek *Chi Rho* (the first letters of 'Christ'). The crossed keys of the Roman papacy would later imitate the *Chi Rho,* but with one difference: that each key also copied the shape of the *fasces* – the bundles of rods and axes carried by the *lictors* (attendants or magistrates) in Imperial Rome to symbolise the authority of the law.

With regard to Andrew's apostolic activity, the most reliable source is the first Church historian, Eusebius (who states that Scythia – southern Russia – was assigned to Andrew). After Andrew's death, the city of Sinope, which he is said to have visited, proudly claimed to have an *ambo* (pulpit) from which Andrew preached.

The stories of Andrew's visit to Russia and the conversion of Bravlin are also to be found in one of the first entries in *The Tale of Bygone Years* (or *Primary Chronicle*). The *Chronicle* is thought to have been compiled between AD 1100-1200 by two Kievan monks, Nestor and Sylvestor, using older annals and legends. There it is claimed that Andrew, while teaching and preaching in the Greek colony of Sinope, set off to go to Rome via Cherson in the Crimea, the Dnieper river, the land of the Slovenians and Scandinavia.

His first stop (the *Chronicle* tells us) was at the place now known as the city of Kiev. There he raised a wooden cross on the surrounding hills, baptising the land and promising that one day it would be Christian. He predicted the construction of a great town full of churches. When Andrew journeyed on to Slovenian territory, he arrived at the site of the future city of Novgorod.

As an observant traveller, Andrew is supposed to have been intrigued by the Slovenian custom of taking sauna baths. These were taken in wooden huts, followed by whippings with thin branches of trees and final showers of cold water.

Many of these more or less legendary accounts of Andrew's missionary activities probably originated in Egypt and Syria and from there were introduced into Byzantine ecclesiastical circles.

Their main source was probably a report of Andrew's apostolic activity that can ultimately be traced to the Apocrypha generally regarded as of heretical, often Gnostic in origin and which, from the fourth century onwards, were often rejected by the Church Fathers. They were composed in the second or at the beginning of the third century, probably written in Greek in *Achaea* (Greece) or by an Egyptian.

Gnostics (from the Greek *gnosis* – knowledge) believed that they, and they alone, had a special revelation from God which would ensure their salvation. For the Gnostics, the physical parts of God's Creation were evil. In their view, Christ was God but was not human; he had been sent to rescue particles of spirit (souls) trapped in matter. Hence, the *Acts of Andrew's* exaggerated emphasis on Andrew's rejection of the values and cultures he came across in his mission.

Only a short text of the original *Acts of Andrew* is preserved in a Greek manuscript in the Vatican Library. But the *Acts of Andrew* survived, at least in part, in some western and eastern adaptations – including Ethiopian and Coptic texts from Africa.

Chapter 3

CONSTANTINE
THE GREAT

A S already suggested, one of the engaging aspects of Andrew was that he was a very malleable saint, whose story could be fairly easily adapted to communicate whatever contemporary message was needed. The lives of the saints were important to the developing Christian Church and Christian society as signposts on the long march to salvation. Andrew provided an indisputable apostolic root and a genealogical route to Christ through Peter. This provided the Church not only with doctrinal authenticity and continuity of priestly ordination, but also, when necessary, with political and military credibility.

Andrew's was a pro-active life of conspicuous virtue, not one of mere passive holiness. In addition he had the advantage of having, evidently, travelled widely. But, unlike Paul of Tarsus, Andrew left no personal correspondence or developed moral teaching.

In the course of time, Andrew developed into a highly-charged symbol rather than a simply historic figure – a pliable but, nevertheless, most effective exemplar of Christian strength of character and tenacity of purpose.

The next most significant event in the development of the persuasive myth of Andrew took place on 28 October AD 312, on the outskirts of Rome. The central role of the cult of Andrew in Scottish history cannot be understood without reference to the battle fought between the emperors Constantine I and Maxentius, at the Milvian Bridge over the River Tiber on the northern approach to Rome.

Constantine, of course, had proven historical links with Britain. Although early English historians would later suggest that Constantine was born in Colchester and that his grandfather was King Coel ('Old King Cole'), he was in all probability born at Naissus in the Danube valley. His mother Helena (who was believed to have discovered the Cross of Christ in Jerusalem in AD 326) accompanied his father Constantius (who may have been a Christian and was certainly sympathetic to them) on his last campaign to Britain to push the Picts back beyond Hadrian's Wall. When Constantius died at York on 25 July AD 306, his son Constantine was with him.

On his father's death, the army hailed Constantine as Augustus, the embodiment of the sun-god, and dressed him in the imperial purple

Six years later, although the odds were against him, Constantine began his campaign from Gaul across the Alps into Italy. He set his sights on Rome. Standing between Constantine and undisputed control of the western Empire was his fellow-emperor, Maxentius, whose enemies branded him a tyrant. Constantine, nonetheless, was determined to become emperor of the Roman Empire in the West.

Constantine was not a Christian. In his search for religious legitimisation he had already put his trust first of all in the god Hercules, then changed his allegiance to the god Apollo.

Writing a quarter of a century after the event, Eusebius, the historian and Bishop of Caesarea, explained that Constantine realised that he needed not only military power to defeat Maxentius, but the assistance of an additional and unexpected force to counteract Maxentius who had enlisted the help of black magicians and psychic powers.

Maxentius had been reported as having consulted the Sibylline oracle's books before the battle. These were the supposedly divinely-inspired prophecies of the Sibyl of Cumae, near Naples, which were preserved on the Temple of Jupiter on the Capitoline Hill and consulted in national emergencies.

The prophecy Maxentius received was as follows: 'On this day, the enemy of Rome will die.' Maxentius, a senior emperor, had persecuted the Christians. He was as superstitious as Constantine but, unlike the latter, was reputed to have indulged in sexual excesses.

Initially Constantine was far from being a convert to Christianity, even though there are clear indications that his mother, and perhaps also his father, were Christians. Indeed it was not until he was on the point of death in AD 337 that Constantine was baptised.

At first, Constantine was not convinced of the validity of Christ, but quite cynically and for purely self-seeking motives, he decided to test the strength of Christ as a means of securing victory on the battle-field. In this Constantine was as pragmatic as Moses. If he won, he would give his allegiance to Christ; if he lost, he would take it as a sign that the Christian God was not supreme.

While the Battle of Milvian Bridge was evidently part of a struggle for secular power, it would, given the benefit of hindsight, later be seen as an affirmation of Christ's divinity.

The assault on Maxentius would become not just a campaign to put down a rebellion, but the first historical crusade. Although Constantine claimed to believe in Christ's power, it needed an extraordinary vision to convince him.

According to Eusebius, God heard Constantine's prayer for victory and sent him a sign in the sky. Above the setting sun the Emperor and his army saw the Greek letters *Chi Rho* clearly outlined in the sky by the blazing red and gold refraction of the rays of the setting sun as it sank down into the horizon. The significance of the sign was that Constantine would conquer only if he adopted the *Chi Rho* as his insignia.

Constantine did not at first understand what was behind the meaning of this splendid and blinding sunset. Certainly it was of more significance than the rural wisdom of observations along the lines of 'Red sky at night, shepherd's delight'. But Constantine only grasped its deeper meaning when he had fallen asleep and started dreaming about Christ. In his dream, Christ urged him to use the sign he had seen in the sky when he went into battle.

When Constantine awoke early in the morning of 28 October, he called for the Christian priests. They explained that the *Chi Rho* was the symbol of Christ's victory over death (the letters also form a crude stick-man with a head and outstretched limbs), and instructed him in the central truths of the Christian faith.

Constantine immediately gave orders to fly the *Chi Rho* on a cavalry standard at the head of his army. He commanded that the same letters be painted on the shields of his soldiers and then had a golden *Chi Rho* soldered onto his own helmet.

In later times Constantine was to display a more ornate standard. The *Labarum* – as the new Christian standard was called – would be made from a long spear wrapped in gold with a cross-bar to form the shape of the Cross of Christ. On the spear-head a golden ceremonial wreath studded with gems was placed. In the middle of the wreath was the *Chi Rho*. From the cross-bar flew a cloth woven from golden thread and richly embroidered; while between the wreath and the banner were the portraits of Constantine and his family, in sheets of beaten gold.

As the moment of battle approached, Constantine's opponent Maxentius had made the most of his position. Central to his defence was the Milvian Bridge, built in 109 BC over the River Tiber at the northern approaches to Rome by the censor M. Aemilius Scaurua. The Milvian Bridge already had some political significance, as it was there that Cicero captured the emissaries of the Allobroges in 63 BC during the Catiline conspiracy.

Between the bridge and the city, two miles to the south, Maxentius had constructed a complex system of forts and trenches to supplement the protection of the city walls. Close to the bridge he built a sturdy pontoon of boats lashed together to provide additional access for his forces. He was secure in the overwhelming superiority of his army and had also taken good care that the old gods and the oracles were on his side.

The battle began and raged fiercely. However, against all the odds, Maxentius' men were forced back to the Milvian Bridge. Soon, it became too narrow for the soldiers trying to withdraw across it. They made for the alternative route – the new floating bridge. Then, at the height of the fighting, the ropes holding the pontoon of boats together gave way unexpectedly under the enormous pressure of retreating men. Hundreds of soldiers from the defending army were thrown into the water, Maxentius among them.

Eusebius compares the confusion of this moment to the scene in the book of Exodus where Pharaoh and the Egyptian army are swallowed up by the waters of the Red Sea – 'they sank like a stone' (Exodus 15:5). Seeing this, the victors' jubilant song of triumph rose to the skies.

Maxentius' body was found later, thrown up at the side of the river. The lifeless head was cut off, impaled on the point of a lance and given pride of place in Constantine's triumphal entry into Rome. Allegiance to Christ had little effect on the ruthlessness of the victor, schooled in the discipline of the Roman army. Constantine needed to demonstrate unequivocally to the Roman people the completeness of his victory and the beginning of a new era.

For Constantine, the Battle of Milvian Bridge was a moment of considerable personal conversion. It was the start of a new covenant which would see Christianity adopted as the state religion because Constantine had discovered by hard personal experience that Christ brought military victory and economic success. For Constantine himself, the defeat of Maxentius placed Constantine at the head of the western half of the Roman Empire.

The Milvian Bridge would, in later centuries, hold a special significicance for the whole Christian Church, as it marked the defeat of the old gods and their mysteries and the ascendancy of the new Christian religion of Light. The Sun had become identified with the Son.

One of Constantine's priorities was to rebuild Rome as a fitting capital where Heaven could touch Earth. Among the many projects was the basilica built over the shrine of St Peter (completed in AD 349 after Constantine's death). Twelve years later, after defeating the Eastern emperor Licinus, Constantine became sole emperor.

On 8 November AD 324, Constantine renamed the ancient eastern capital of Byzantium. He called it 'Constantinople'. There, on the site of what would later become the Church of the Holy Apostles, he erected a circular mausoleum for his own burial.

After Constantine's death in AD 337, his body was duly interred in the mausoleum. Twenty years later, Constantine's son, the emperor Constantius II, built a cruciform basilica next to it where he deposited the relics of the Apostles Timothy (AD 356) and Luke and Andrew (AD 357), the latter from Patras. These had been forcibly collected by armed agents of Constantius and would have almost certainly involved considerable outrage among the communities who saw their traditional centres of piety and income from pilgrims brutally eradicated.

In spite of the emperor's orders, it would appear that, in the case of Patras at least, some parts of the body of Andrew were secretly removed by the local clergy – notably (as later events would suggest) the head. Whether this implies that an alternative skull was substituted, is not clear.

It is possible that the mummified body, wrapped in linen and perhaps contained in a wooden coffin, may have been uplifted by Constantius' agents, without checking that all its constituent parts were present – it might have been possible to replace the real skull with a substitute.

The Scottish historian, the Augustinian abbot Walter Bower, writing on the island of Inchcolm in the 1440s, with the benefit of hindsight, has his St Regulus spiriting away quite other parts of the saint's skeleton: ' … three fingers of the right hand, the arm-bone that hangs down from the shoulder, one tooth and a knee-cap.'

Although it seems that some parts of the body were kept hidden in Patras, the older Graeco-Roman and the much later Scottish accounts differ radically as to which parts of the skeleton were concerned.

Certainly, it seems likely that the skeleton of the saint would not have been washed and de-articulated until some time after it reached Constantinople. There it would receive the attentions of the most sophisticated reliquary-technicians of the day, skilled in the art of making as many relics as possible from the two hundred distinct bones in the human skeleton, so as to support the faith of believers all over the world.

The body of Andrew had been venerated at Patras in the Peloponnesos, where it had been buried, it is said, by Maximilla after being taken down from the cross at the shore. In AD 397 what were claimed to be the relics of the prophet Samuel were also transferred to Constantinople.

Constantius' policy of collecting the bodies of Christian heroes was aimed at increasing the status of the churches in the new capital. It also served to underline the integration of the secular with the religious power.

Although Constantine's body was later moved by his son Constantinus from the original mausoleum to the new Church of the Holy Apostles, St John Chrysostom (Bishop of Constantinople 398-404) confirms that the emperors were buried in the outer vestibule of the Church of the Holy Apostles (not inside it), beside the relics.

The transfer of the relics of Andrew to Constantinople was in no way regarded in the West or in Rome as a challenge to the Imperial City which already had the relics of Peter and Paul. However, in later centuries, when Constantinople sought to rival Rome, it was to become a challenge.

Essentially, 'relics' were the mortal remains of holy persons, or objects sanctified by contact with them. The first relics venerated by Christians were those of the Martyrs who were tortured and put to death until persecution ended in AD 312. 'Primary relics' (parts of the bodies of saints) were venerated as signs of the victory of Christ's sacrificial death repeated in the death of his saints. 'Secondary relics' (cloth which had been placed over the bodies of the saints accompanied by the most solemn prayers and known as *brandea*), were at first opposed but eventually accepted as instruments through which God had chosen to work.

From the fourth century onwards, bodies of those considered to be saints were exhumed, dismembered and distributed to various local churches, especially to Alexandria, Antioch and Constantinople. Constantinople, a newcomer with few native martyrs' remains from the pre-Constantinian persecutions, worked hard at gathering relics.

Among the vast collection of relics brought to Constantinople were the Instruments of the Passion: two pieces of the True Cross; the Pillar at which Jesus was scourged; the Crown of Thorns; the Sponge and the Sacred Lance used to pierce Christ's side.

The cult of relics developed from an established belief in the power of *virtue* (from the Latin *virtus*). *Virtus* is used in the Gospels on only few occasions. It refers to the healing influence of Jesus, such as was shown in the case of the woman who had suffered for twelve years from an issue of blood (Luke 8:43-50); or the preaching of Jesus to those who had come to him to be healed from disease (Luke 6: 17-19). It is worth recalling that certainly Andrew would almost have been present at the healing miracles which Jesus performed by touching the sick person: 'When the local people recognised him, they spread the news through the whole neighbourhood and took all that were sick to him, begging him just to let them touch the fringe of his cloak. And all those who touched it were completely cured' (Matthew 14:34).

Specific cures of this nature include the healing of the deaf man (Mark 8:31); the blind man at Bethsaida, Andrew's own town (Mark 8:22); the man suffering from leprosy (Luke 5:12); the woman suffering from a haemorrhage (Luke 8:40); the crippled woman (Luke 7:10); the son of the widow of Nain (Luke 7·11).

The healing power of the words of Jesus nevertheless required an act of believing self-surrender on the part of those who came to be healed. It was not magic but a two-way process. The display and veneration of relics were a powerful mechanism for regenerating a sense of commitment and motivation in the believer.

One would hesitate to say that an 'industry' in the presentation of relics gradually arose. Certainly it was a highly-specialised task which required all the skills of the undertaker, the anatomist and the priest.

The original tombs of the saints would be reverently unearthed and opened many years after their death, when only the bare skeleton would be left in the grave. The bones of the saints (the *corporeal* relics) would normally be washed as a disarticulated skeleton of more than 200 separate bones. Then they would be wrapped and replaced in a new container at ground level, a secondary coffin which formed the core of the shrine. This process of enshrinement was known as *translatio* ('translation') or *commutatio*. These visible burial-places of the martyrs played a vital part in the development of the early Church and the 'translation' (deposition) of relics was often celebrated annually as a special feast-day.

In Italy the initiator of the cult of the Apostles was St Ambrose (who built a church in Milan dedicated to the Apostles). At that church he placed relics of Andrew, John and Thomas which he had obtained from Constantinople. The deposition of the relics was commemorated annually in May.

Even at this early period, other Italian cities already claimed relics of Andrew. Paulinus, Bishop of Nola (who was born in AD 353 near Bordeaux, became Bishop of Nola *circa* 409 and died in 431), is found congratulating himself for having obtained parts relics of Andrew and Luke for his basilicas in Nola and Fondi. The city of Concordia in Lombardy also possessed some souvenirs of the Apostles, including some of Andrew.

Gaudentius of Brescia, who died *circa* 410, writes that Andrew was greatly venerated in the Western Church in his day. He boasts that his church in Brescia contains relics of John the Baptist, Andrew, Thomas and Luke. He apparently also obtained his relics from St Ambrose.

In Ravenna there were fifth century monuments dedicated to Andrew. Theodoric the Great, King of the Ostrogoths, ruler of Italy (493-526), built a church (destroyed in 1457) in the name of Andrew and dedicated it to the cult of the Goths. The Goths seem to have had a particular veneration to Andrew. His feast is commemorated on 29 November in a fifth century Gothic calendar composed in Thrace. And Petrus Chrysologus of Ravenna, who died in 450, commemorated Andrew's feast day in a sermon in which he confirmed that the saint was crucified on a tree.

In Ravenna also, in his own palace, Bishop Peter II (494-519) built a chapel dedicated to St Andrew; while Bishop Maximian (died 546) restored the church of St Andrew and placed more relics there brought from Constantinople. Maximian must have been in Constantinople soon after 548 when, during the demolition of the old basilica, relics of Andrew, Luke and Timothy were rediscovered and placed in the new building constructed by the emperor Justinian.

Maximian wanted to take the body of St Andrew to Ravenna, but the Emperor was determined that the New Rome must continue to possess the relics of St Peter's brother. However, by a ruse, Maximian succeeded in obtaining what was said to be the beard of St Andrew which he transported to Ravenna.

In Rome the feast of St Andrew was celebrated in the fourth century, preceded by a vigil and fasting. The cult of St Andrew grew in Rome particularly during the Acacian Schism (AD 485-519) – a split in the Church between East and West over the nature of Christ.

The first Roman basilica in honour dedicated to St Andrew was erected on the Esquiline Hill by Pope Simplicius (468-483). Pope Gelasius I (492-496) also built an oratory in honour of St Andrew on the Via Labicana. Near the basilica of St Peter, Pope Symachus (498-514) constructed a rotunda dedicated to St Andrew.

In Gaul, St Victricius, Bishop of Rouen who died at start of the fifth century, mentions the deposition of relics of Thomas, Andrew and Luke in his cathedral. According to Gregory of Tours (*circa* 538-594), there were relics of St Andrew preserved at Neuvy not far from Tours.

The spread of the St Andrew cult in Rome, Italy and Gaul in the fourth and fifth centuries shows that Westerners were not yet aware of any Byzantine attempt to overshadow or equalise the prestige of Peter with that of his brother.

In the fifth century, copies of the *Acts of Andrew* circulated in the West. Pope Innocent I (402-417) mentions them; while Turibius, a contemporary of Pope Leo the Great (*circa* 390-461), warned the faithful against reading them.

For later centuries, much of the popularity of St Andrew is due to the Frankish historian Gregory, Bishop of Tours (who edited a book about the achievements of Andrew). Leaving aside the many stories he considered to be exaggerated (and therefore heretical), he chose some of the miracles of Andrew and the adventures he experienced along the shores of the Black Sea. Andrew had become a folk hero in the mould of Sinbad the Sailor.

Gregory of Tours, among many colourful stories about Andrew the Apostle, also recounted the unlikely miracle which cured a certain Mammolus who, in the sixth century decided to visit Andrew's tomb to be cured of prostate trouble – mainly his inability to pass water. The saint, according to Gregory, answered Mammolus' prayers and he eventually passed a colossal stone!

There had been, up to this period, however, no attempt to connect Andrew with the beginnings of Christianity in Byzantium through the person of Stachys, whom Andrew was supposed to have instituted as Bishop of Byzantium. Nor is there any evidence that Andrew was being used (as he would later be) as a figure-head to increase the status of Constantinople to rival that of Rome.

In 573, the future Pope Gregory the Great was *Urban Prefect* (head of the Senate) and, when his father died, one of the richest men in Rome. Within the next twelve months, Gregory transformed his family home on the Coelian Hill into a monastery dedicated to St Andrew, with a style of living loosely based on the Rule of St Benedict (*circa* 480-547). Today, with its oratory of St Andrew, the building is known as San Gregorio Magno.

Gregory went on to found six monasteries in all. Half a century later, in AD 625, Pope Honorius I, perhaps inspired by Gregory's example, also turned his Roman home near the Lateran into a monastery, dedicated, like Gregory's, to St Andrew.

Meanwhile Rome, poorly defended, was an easy prey to the Lombard invaders. Desperate for reinforcements, Pope Pelagius II sent Gregory to Constantinople as papal legate to the new emperor, Mauricius, whose acquaintance Gregory had made while Mauricius was still an officer with a distinguished military career.

From 579 to 586, Gregory served in Constantinople. In his *Dialogues,* he confesses that in order not be too much immersed in secular matters when at Constantinople, he brought with him some monks from his own monastery of St Andrew. Perhaps his desire to remain detached from the exotic society life of Constantinople also explains why Gregory quite unashamedly admitted that, during all his time in the city, he had not learnt to speak a word of Greek.

However, he could not fail to notice the wealth of relics now accumulated in the city. Shortly before he left for Rome, Gregory persuaded the Emperor to give him a number of them for his monastery. Chief among these was the head of St Luke and the arm of St Andrew – 'arm' probably signifying the hand, the lower and upper arm-bones and the shoulder-blade.

When Gregory reported back to Rome, Pope Pelagius II promoted him to secretary of state. Only a year later, Gregory set off on a mission to England but was recalled. In AD 590 Gregory, still only a deacon, was, at the command of the emperor, made Bishop of Rome, assuming the reins of office even before he had been ordained.

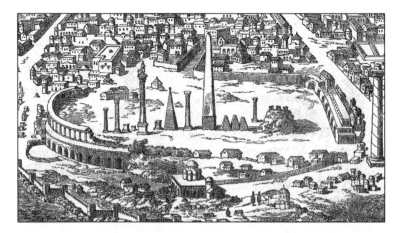

ANCIENT CONSTANTINOPLE

Chapter 4

SAINT
ANDREW
IN ENGLAND

FROM the death of Pope Pelagius II, there had been almost seven months vacancy in the Holy See prior to Gregory's election as pope. Disaster struck Rome: the Church's wheat granaries were swept away by floods and torrential rain. To make matters worse, the city was in the grip of the plague.

Gregory, confirmed in his new office, gave orders for a penitential procession through the city with sung invocations to God and the saints. This took place on three days in succession, the faithful desperately chanting *Kyrie eleison* ('God have mercy'). As they marched, people in the procession could be seen collapsing and dying in the streets.

The hostile elements and scourge of disease which wracked Rome served only to challenge Gregory. He saw himself as the captain of the ship of state and the barque of Peter, struggling to hold his course and reach dry land. He wrote to his friend Leander, Bishop of Seville:

Although battered by the wind and the rain, I do not let go of the rudder ... I turn to face the storm. When the ship lurches to one side I steer through the heaving sea. The stinking cargo of sin which we carry makes me cry out in anguish. I can hear, over the howling gale, the frightening crack of ship's timbers breaking. Wiping back my tears I glimpse the tranquil land of my dreams which I will never see again. As the anger of the hurricane forces me away, I snatch a sight of the shore and groan.

Fundamental to Gregory's understanding of the Church was the belief that it was not only Holy and Catholic, but *Apostolic* – of Apostolic foundation, and connected to the Apostles by an uninterrupted episcopal succession. Central, in this respect, was the conviction that the Church's dogmas were based on the teaching of the Apostles which, in turn, derived directly from Christ.

19

'*Non angli sed angeli* – not Angles but angels': this famous play on words is said to have been delivered by Gregory five years later, when, in the autumn of AD 595, he came upon slaves from Britain standing in the market-place. Gregory was so struck by the noble savagery of their appearance that he ordered the 17 and 18 year old youths to be purchased by the Church and placed in monasteries at Rome to be trained for the service of God. His intention was that one day they should be sent back to their homeland as missionaries.

The Angles were originally a Germanic tribe from the Angeln district of Schelswig who, together with the Saxons and Jutes, had invaded and conquered most of England during the fifth century AD.

Gregory had been approached by Christians among the Angles who asked him to send out missionaries, as the local bishops made no effort to preach the Gospel to them. He invited forty of the monks from his monastery of St Andrew to go as missionaries to Britain led by Augustine. They left Rome in the spring of 596 and reached Provence in France. Morale among the monks was not high, so Augustine returned to Rome and was given a letter by Gregory. 'Do not let the difficulty of the journey nor the evil tongues of men alarm you,' he wrote and enclosed letters of introduction to the bishops on their route to Britain.

In France, the missionaries were joined by a number of local priests who were to act as interpreters in England.

The historian, the Venerable Bede, tells us that when, just before Easter AD 597, Augustine landed in Kent, King Ethelbert insisted on hearing him in the open air. Gregory's correspondence hints clearly that Augustine landed only when he had been certain of Ethelbert's welcome. The King's wife, Bertha, was a Christian and had helped to ensure that her husband would welcome the missionaries. That Christmas, more than 10,000 Angles were baptised.

Moreover, as Augustine had informed Pope Gregory that he had a great harvest, but few labourers, Gregory sent along an increased supply of fellow-workers and ministers of the word. The most influential personalities among these were Mellitus, Justus, Paulinus and Rufianus. With them Gregory also sent all kinds of things which would be needed for the service of the Church – sacred vessels, altar draperies, church ornaments, vestments for bishops and clergy, relics of some of the holy Apostles and Martyrs, and a supply of books.

Gregory also sent letters to encourage Augustine's missionary team and informed them of a far-sighted policy decision – to incorporate those elements of pagan practice which were acceptable to

Christianity. At the same time, he was anxious to make use of what religious buildings already existed, once they had been suitably cleansed.

'Do not pull down any of the pagan shrines,' he wrote. 'Destroy only the actual images of the pagan gods which they contain. Then bless holy water and sprinkle it over the shrines. Finally, build altars and place relics inside them.'

At Canterbury, Augustine and his monastic community dedicated their first monastery to Saints Peter and Paul, the patron saints of Rome. Later, in AD 604, King Ethelbert erected for them the church of the blessed Apostle Andrew.

St Andrew's Priory, Rochester, a Saxon cathedral which was destroyed at the Norman Conquest, was probably not a stone building. Yet, even in the present (third) cathedral building, St Andrew's Day is still celebrated.

The crypt of Saints Peter and Paul was modelled on that of St Peter's, Rome, which, with that of St Paul, was the shrine to which pilgrimages from the northern nations came most frequently.

The progress of evangelisation often rested on a knife-edge. Making converts was one thing, but keeping them quite another. One of the major problems facing Augustine and his fellow-missionaries was consolidating the faith of those who had been newly baptised.

Much depended on the protection and encouragement of local kings. When Ethelbert died in AD 616 and was buried in St Augustine's Abbey at Canterbury, power was transferred from Kent to Redwald, King of the East Angles.

A backlash against christianisation now threatened the work of Augustine, particularly when there were kings such as Eadbald, who had never been baptised and who had revolted from Christianity. And, shortly after, Seberht, King of the East Saxons, died leaving three sons who soon reverted back to the old religion. Then Bishop Justus of Rochester abandoned his See and retired to Canterbury where he remained for twelve months.

However, reciprocal contact between Britain and Rome grew steadily. As early as AD 726, King Ine of Wessex (the territory of the West Saxons), who died in Rome in the same year, founded the church of San Spirito in Sassia specifically for Saxon pilgrims (which lasted until it was rebuilt in 1540).

In AD 627 a timber church was erected over a spring in the city of York and there on Easter Sunday, King Edwin was baptised. Edwin appointed York, the principal town of Deira, as the see of Paulinus and began to build a basilican church of stone around the wooden oratory.

At Ripon, St Wilfrid's church was said to have been built upon the site of an ancient British church, but it also had a crypt. Hexham, also one of Wilfrid's churches, had a similar crypt'.

Wilfrid, one of key figures in the development of devotion to St Andrew, was born in AD 634 and entered the monastery at Lindisfarne in his teenage years. In 653, with Benedict Biscop, he left for Rome and travelled with him via Lyon. There he was introduced to Pope Eugenius. The pope placed his hand on Wilfrid's head, prayed over him, and blessed him.

In Rome, Wilfrid went round the shrines of the saints with his companions, making a collection of relics, each labelled with the saint's name. He also bought purple cloth and silk vestments to decorate his churches. Then, with the blessing of the saints upon him, Wilfrid set off in the peace of Christ, armed with the holy relics he had collected, and so returned safely to England in 658. After the Synod of Whitby (633) he was elected bishop of Northumbria and consecrated in the Gallican rite at Compiègne in northern France.

By 678, Wilfrid had gained control over extensive territories. King Ecgfrith, alarmed at Wilfrid's growing status, demanded that the diocese be split into four. Wilfrid appealed over Ecgfrith's head to Rome – the first recorded appeal to Rome by an English prelate.

Wilfrid again travelled to Rome, where he won the appeal. On his return to England, however, he was imprisoned and exiled by Ecgfrith.

Ecgfrith had defeated a Pictish revolt around 672 and seems to have secured recognition of his authority even from the Scots of Dal Riata and the Britons of Strathclyde. But in 685 he was killed in battle at Nechtansmere and from that time the hopes and strength of the Northumbrians began to ebb away.

After Ecgfrith's death at Nechtansmere, Wilfrid returned to Hexham, regaining the see of York and the monastery at Ripon.

Once again, in 691, Wilfrid quarrelled (this time with Aldfrith) about land and went to Rome again to fight his case.

Of Wilfrid's church at Hexham, dedicated to St Andrew and constructed (originally of wood) on royal land, no certain trace remains above ground. Only the famous stone crypt survives. Hexham became a cathedral in 678 and was subsequently enlarged by Bishop Acca.

In Hexham, Wilfrid's nave crypt is probably the most famous early crypt still extant in the northern half of Western Europe. The church at Hexham was dedicated to St Andrew by Wilfrid in 674. The relics of the Apostle Andrew were brought there by Acca – either on one of his many visits to Rome or from the relics originally brought over from Gregory's monastery in Rome and placed in St Andrew's, Rochester.

The two Apostles who were to be most steadily and continuously honoured in England were St Andrew and St James. St Andrew is one of six or seven saints common to all the 40 counties of England.

In England there were to be between 600 and 700 churches dedicated to St Andrew. Of these 570 were ancient ones (including the cathedrals of Wells and Rochester). It is also worth noting that in pre-Reformation England there were only 106 churches dedicated to St George.

Wilfrid had proceeded with the erection of churches in the northern portion of his see which extended to the Forth. Indeed, he regarded the Picts as being under his special charge. When Wilfrid fell into disfavour, he was imprisoned for a time in Dunbar in East Lothian.

In Rome in 680, Wilfrid had spoken publicly on behalf of the Picts, declaring them to be faithful children of the Church. Accordingly, in the following year, a separate bishop of the Picts was appointed, who took Abercorn in Linlithgowshire as his seat.

After the battle of Nechtansmere at Dunnichen (685), the church of North Britain was finally separated from that of the south.

Wilfrid died at Ripon in AD 709.

HEXHAM ABBEY

23

Chapter 5

THE RELICS
GO NORTH

ALTHOUGH the aim of the original Augustinian mission to Kent had been to introduce Christianity through persuasion and example, Pope Gregory (perhaps remembering the very real military threat which had led in AD 579 to his own posting to Constantinople) did not hesitate from advocating, when necessary, the use of warfare as a forcible method of conversion.

The pagan rulers of England were sympathetic to the concept of a 'holy war' or 'crusade ethic' because belief in the God of the Christians evidently held out the proven promise of a better-than-even chance of victory in battle.

In this they were not much different to the Emperor Constantine when he became convinced that he needed to embrace the insignia of Christianity at the Milvian Bridge. It was certainly a pragmatic and self-seeking reason for fighting under the flag of Christ, but apparently immensely practical, in that it achieved the desired result.

In seventh and eighth century Britain it was not outwith the realms of possibility that Christian spirituality could motivate effectively precisely because the Augustinian mission (and all it implied) brought with it a revitalised vision of Christ, straight from the monastic community of the new and dynamic pope – Gregory. In addition, the old pagan beliefs had perhaps become tired from long familiarity and were failing to grip the imagination of their adherents.

As the resurgence of Christian belief moved north from Kent, it gained momentum from the activities of bishops such as Acca, the litigious Wilfrid's chaplain in the last years of his life, and his close companion. On Wilfrid's death in 709, Acca succeeded him as Bishop of Hexham, and enlarged and enriched his church at St Andrew's, Hexham, collecting yet more relics of the saints, building up a library, teaching liturgical music and using his wide experience as a theologian to explain and promote the Christian faith.

The Venerable Bede held Acca in great regard, dedicating a number of books to him, some of which Acca had also commissioned. But, in spite of all his gifts and achievements, Acca was suddenly and inexplicably expelled from his see, never to return.

It is possible that Acca was in some way caught up in the dynastic conflict following attempts to depose the local King Ceolwulf, who would himself later abdicate to become a monk at Lindisfarne. Acca had been a staunch supporter of Ceolwulf and may even have been a relative. When the latter was forced out of office in 731, Acca seems to have been one of the immediate casualties.

According to Simeon of Durham, Acca was driven from his see in AD 731 or 732. Rumour had it at the time that he had gone to found a bishop's see among the Picts. There is also a suggestion that Acca may even have stayed for some time in the south-west of Scotland at Whithorn in Galloway.

Only a few years after Acca's forced departure from Hexham, the bishopric of St Andrews was founded by a Pictish king called Óengus. It is not certain which Pictish king this was – either Óengus I, son of Fergus (729–61) or Óengus II (820–34). In both cases, they were Pictish warlords and over-kings of the kingdom of Fortriu (southern Perthshire). While no direct link can be proved between the two events, a connection between them seems highly likely.

Acca's exile and consequent search for royal patronage provides the strong motivating opportunity and the availability of the Apostle's relics; a royal monastic foundation at Kilrymont in Fife is historical fact and the location of Andrew's relics at Kilrymont was certainly accepted common belief.

The cult of Andrew the Apostle had, after all, accompanied the corporeal and non-corporeal relics of the saint. The former had moved steadily northwards from Patras to Constantinople; to Rome (and, later, to Amalfi), and so finally, through Canterbury, Rochester and Hexham, to Scotland.

The primary function of new religious foundations was to underpin royal dynasties. Political circumstances immediately north and south of the Firth of Forth were becoming receptive to such foundations. Supreme kings were emerging to weld smaller monarchies together. Economies of scale were in evidence as territories and possessions were forcibly merged through aggressive military expeditions.

This general process was taking place in the eighth and ninth centuries as ethnic groupings were forced together by Pictish supreme kings. This was accompanied by the development of the cult of different saints and the elaboration of genealogies of the kings to justify their right of inheritance.

In the Early Church, a 'saint' had first been a member of the baptised church or the faithful departed. Gradually the term was extended to cover the martyrs.

Where Scotland in the eighth century was concerned, the saint whose heroic missionary endeavours still resonated most strongly was Columba (521-97), the Irish Apostle of Christianity, raised in the royal warrior aristocracy of Donegal. Columba's monastery on the island of Iona became the mother church of Celtic Christianity in Scotland. Other saints, such as Ninian (fl 390), the earliest known Christian leader in Scotland, were widely venerated.

In the eighth century, the church of the Picts had first identified itself with St Peter as its chief patronal saint, perhaps in the reign of Nechtan (king circa 600-30), and finally with St Andrew, possibly during the reign of Óengus I. Both kings ruled for a long and reasonably stable period.

During the reigns of Nechtan and Óengus, and also that of Constantine (789-820), attempts were increasingly made to model the role of the king on that of the Roman emperor, Constantine the Great. In all, there were four kings named after him: Constantine, King of the Picts (789-820); and three kings of Alba – Constantine I (862-79), Constantine II (900-40) and Constantine III (995-97).

In western Europe, after about the year 750, especially in the life of the Holy Roman Emperor Charlemagne (747-814), the Constantinian model grew in importance.

Charlemagne had subdued and christianized the kingdoms around him, especially those of the Saxons and Lombards. The exploits of his chief paladin, Roland, had produced the heroic literature of the *Chanson de Roland*. In AD 800, Charlemagne marched his armies to Rome in support of Pope Leo III, who in gratitude crowned him Emperor of the Romans in St Peter's basilica. But warfare was no more than a necessary evil. Charlemagne's administration was also characterised by effective and just laws, by stability and peace, all assured by military supremacy.

Charlemagne encouraged the growth of education, agriculture, industry and commerce. For the Pictish kings – and later the Scots – this made his achievement well worth imitating as far as practicable on the much smaller scale of the Scottish mainland.

Out of the many conflicting accounts which surround the growth of the cult of Andrew, there are two key events upon which all the historical records broadly agree. First, somewhere south of the Firth of Forth, a Pictish king was motivated by belief in Saint Andrew to conquer in battle. Second, a Pictish king encouraged and supported the establishment of a shrine to Andrew the Apostle at what was to become St Andrews in Fife. It is not at all clear whether the two events were or were not directly connected, or whether the two Pictish kings were one and the same person.

There are two main versions of these events and several subsidiary ones. They attempt to explain the significance of what happened by linking the battle story to the foundation legend.

No eye-witness accounts survive either of the battle or foundation. The first existing version is in a late twelfth century manuscript, once part of the library of the Cistercian abbey at Newminster in Northumberland. Another was written at York around 1360.

The second version survives in an eighteenth century copy of a lost St Andrews manuscript. Another, stolen to order from St Andrews by a German collector around the time of the Reformation, dates from the fourteenth century. Hence, the earliest versions we have of the incidents surrounding the foundation of the shrine at St Andrews were written about six hundred years after the events themselves – although they may well have been taken from earlier manuscripts which no longer exist.

The first version was probably written at St Andrews in the royal hall, perhaps by a Culdee (*cèli dè* – 'companions of God') monk. It appears to be a sermon for St Andrew's Day, and may have been based on previous homilies written not later than the early twelfth century.

The second version of the story claims to have been composed for King Ferath, son of Bargoit, who reigned *circa* 840. However, it is more likely to have been written in the eleventh or twelfth century. The two versions share a basic storyline but differ in details.

The common thread of the story is as follows: first, the relics of Andrew are forcibly removed from Patras to Constantinople by royal command; second, a Pictish king is victorious in battle through the intervention of Andrew; third, some bones of the saint are taken by a monk from their resting-place; fourth, the bones are carried to Cennrigmonaid (in Scots, *Kilrymont*); fifth, the monk and a king co-operate to found a church dedicated to Andrew the Apostle.

In the first version, we are presented with a king called Óengus I, son of Fergus. Prior to doing battle, he observes a blinding flash of light and hears the voice of Andrew. He is victorious with the saint's help.

The second version was used by John of Fordun in his *Chronica gentis scotorum* (1384-7). Fordun (died *circa* 1384) is thought to have been a chantry priest in Aberdeen. The *Chronica gentis scotorum* is the chief authority for the history of Scotland prior to the fifteenth century. He brought the history down to 1153, but left collections extending to 1383 which were added to and completed by Walter Bower (*circa* 1385-1449), an Augustinian canon.

From 1440-7 Bower compiled what came to be known as the *Scotichronicon,* continuing the story of Scotland to the death of James I in 1437. Of Bower's 16 books, the first five and more are mainly by Fordun.

Walter Bower was born in Haddington and entered the community at the cathedral priory of St Andrews in his early teens. He records the foundation of the University of St Andrews in 1410 and it is assumed that his degree, Bachelor of Decrees, was from the new university. He was appointed Abbot of Inchcolm in 1417 and remained there for over 30 years. It was on the island in the Firth of Forth that he wrote the *Scotichronicon.*

While folk mythology may have speculated about the origins of the Scots, the Venerable Bede's opinion had been that the nation of the Scots had come from Scythia (Ukraine), one of the territories supposed to have been evangelised by St Andrew.

Walter Bower, on the other hand, also proposed that the Scots were descended from the Egyptian Gaytheolos and his wife Scota, daughter of the Pharaoh Chencres who had died in the Red Sea while pursuing the Israelites. This may partly explain the biblical echoes which are frequently to be found in descriptions of the Pictish King Óengus and the Greek St Rule (also known as *Regulus*).

In other words, there was on the one hand some residual folk memory that races and peoples had migrated over the centuries from the Middle East to the north of Europe. But historians also took great care to establish the authenticity of kinship between mythological or biblical figures and the people of the contemporary world. They were trying to show connections between the forgotten past and the dangerous present – trying to provide evidence of the brotherhood of man and the continuity of God's Creation.

The second and awkwardly-linked part of the legend, concerns the Pictish King Óengus. At the same time as St Rule reaches Muckross in Fife, the Apostle appears to the Pictish King Óengus and promises victory to his enemies.

The first version of the legend tells us that Óengus was conducting a military campaign in the northeast of England with mindless destruction and the utmost barbarity – the implication is that he is not at this point a Christian.

He rests up with his troops in the Merse but is soon surrounded by a force drawn from all the nations in Britain, who have one aim in mind – to put him and his whole army to death.

The second version of the legend (and Walter Bower's account in the *Scotichronicon*) has St Andrew appear to Óengus while he is asleep. In the first version, Óengus is walking with his seven closest advisers when they are inexplicably covered with a supernatural luminosity. They fall flat on their faces on the ground and hear a voice from the sky saying 'Óengus, Óengus, listen to me – Andrew, an Apostle of Christ, I am sent by God to defend and guard you. Just look for the sign of the Cross of Christ in the air where it advances against the opposing army. Make a donation of a tenth of your possessions both as a sign of gratitude to Almighty God and in honour of St Andrew'.

According to the first version of the legend, Óengus divides his troops into twelve units. In front of each unit was carried a standard displaying the Cross of Christ, from the tip of which shone an unearthly light.

Later, after the battle, the entry in Bishop William Elphinstone's (*circa* 1431–1514) *Aberdeen Breviary* for the feast of St Regulus records that, at Kilrymont, Óengus was baptised by Regulus. Taken with previous suggestions that he waged war with extreme and unnecessary cruelty, we are justified in concluding that Óengus, like Constantine (but for different reasons), was not a Christian at the time of the battle of Athelstaneford. Constantine, after all, was not baptised until 16 years after the battle of Milvian Bridge – when he was at death's door.

The battle at Athelstaneford, like the battle at the Milvian Bridge for Roman civilisation, was a water-shed in Scottish history, the symbol and sign of a decisive turning-point where Christianity finally succeeded in winning over the most influential royal, civic and military backing.

While there is little doubt that a battle or series of skirmishes similar to Athelstaneford took place at some date and at some place, we are, with the foundation of the church at Kilrymont, on much surer ground, since it refers to an easily-recognisable institution – what became eventually the great cathedral church of St Andrews. The geographical location of the battle, however, is in some respects relatively insignificant. There are no major towns or buildings associated with the battle, only those of a hamlet and a small stream.

The location for the battle specified in the first account is Mercia (central England south of the Humber between Wales and East Anglia), rather than the prevalent interpretation in Scotland as being the Merse (the low-lying land between Lammermuir and Tweed).

If Athelstaneford was indeed the location of Óengus' crucial battle, then it may have had some strategic significance as being on a route from England to the fortress at what would later become Edinburgh.

The modern village of Athelstaneford is 262 metres above sea-level. It lies two miles north of the River Tyne and borders a plain surrounded by fortified hill-tops.

Three thousand metres to the northwest, beyond Kilduff Hill, is the Iron Age hillfort at Chesters, defended by an elaborate system of ramparts and ditches. At a similar distance to the west are the Garleton Hills (highest point Skid Hill at 610 metres), with another hillfort looking east.

About six thousand metres to the southeast is the important hillfort of Traprain Law, which flourished during the Roman occupation between AD 78 and 215. To the east is Markle, said to be a corruption of 'miracle' and supposed to mark the place where the Cross of Christ was seen in the sky.

The Cogtail Burn rises in the Garleton Hills to the west in the valley just below Athelstaneford, running under the Cogtail Bridge until it emerges into the Firth of Forth. Beside the Burn, a long cist Christian burial was found. Just above the bank of the Burn is the Hanging Craig and not far south again, the remains of another hillfort.

There are several contradictions in the accounts of the battle. John of Fordun identifies the hostile leader as Athelstan who outlived Óengus II by several years. However, there may be confusion here with the enemy of Scots – the King of Wessex. In the second version, the enemy is a King of the Saxons called Adelstan, who is beheaded after his defeat by the Picts.

Some historians place the battle during the reign of Óengus I and identify the opposing king as Eadbert whose general was Athelstan. Alternatively, the hostile king may have been the Athelstan who ruled nearly all England south of the Humber and who, in AD 934, planned to conquer the lands to the north. He managed to penetrate as far as Dunfoether (Traprain Law).

Turning to the location of the battle, Fordun translates this from the Latin as Tynemouth in Northumbria, while Walter Bower in the *Scotichronicon* puts the site at Athelstaneford in East Lothian.

The place name, 'Athelstaneford' may come from the Pictish *Aith-ail* [stone-ford] – 'stepping-stones'. This might have been later added to the Anglian equivalent 'staneford' to give 'Athelstaneford'.

The spot where the defeated Athelstan was pulled off his horse and killed was next to the little stream now known as the Cogtail Burn, previously called the Rugdown or Lugdown from the Scots word *rug* (to pull). The vision of the Cross of Christ was reputed to have been to the east, over Markle Farm – the name of the farm assumed to be a corruption of the word 'miracle'.

It is worth remembering that Walter Bower himself was born in Haddington and would have probably visited the site of the battle on several occasions as a boy and perhaps later also, when preparing the text of the *Scotichronicon*.

In the *Scotichronicon*, while explaining that there were three English kings called Athelstan, Walter Bower includes a long quotation from the English chronicler, William of Malmesbury (*circa* 1090-1143) to support his assertion.

He goes on to say in passing that the death of Athelstan at the hands of Óengus is still fresh in his readers' memory, both from a variety of historic documents and from a tradition of oral history that was still alive in his day. It is this oral tradition in particular that Bower can have been expected to have absorbed most vividly during his childhood and schooling in Haddington.

Of course that is not to say that everything Bower has to say about the battle of Athelstaneford is necessarily totally accurate. What it does underline is that Bower's sources were not confined to manuscripts alone, but included his own experience of a living oral tradition in East Lothian and, probably, interviews he may have conducted as part of the information-gathering process for the *Scotichronicon*.

Bower writes that Óengus, at the height of a campaign against the Angle monarchy (in which he and his army had caused immense devastation in Northumbria), decided to set up camp two miles from Haddington on a fertile plain half a mile above what is now the village of Athelstaneford. His intention was to give his army time to replenish supplies and rest after their exertions.

The location he had chosen had abundant fields of corn and grass, woodland shrubs, springs and rivers. It was also on an eminence (which would give him plenty of warning of attack) and was well sheltered, with abundant look-out points at the hillforts to the north and to the west. From the description we can assume that the time of the year was late summer.

Meanwhile, Athelstan assembled a large force and caught Óengus off guard, surrounding the much smaller army of the Picts. Fear and deep pessimism gripped Óengus and his generals. They understood only too well that there was no way of escape. The only thing they could do was to pray.

Speaking in his capacity as a senior cleric, Walter Bower adds that God never fails to help those who sincerely ask for divine assistance. Accordingly, Óengus and representatives of all the ranks of his army made vows to God and the saints, especially Andrew the Apostle.

This suggests that Óengus was already predisposed to accept Christianity, even if only a superficial level. However, Bower does not shirk from describing Óengus's campaign as one of immense (and unnecessary) savagery and brutality, which implies that he was not a Christian before the battle of Athelstaneford. For example, the text of the *Aberdeen Breviary* for 9 May (the Translation of the bones of St Andrew), indicates that Óengus had enemies within his own Pictish ranks. He is said to have executed some of his lords and have faced a conspiracy by others.

On the other hand, we can conclude that some devotion to Andrew was already established among the Picts. Moreover, Óengus, having greater abundance of physical possessions than those who served him, is persuaded to make a solemn promise that if he and his army returned safely to his own territory and he himself was unharmed, then he would in exchange give a tenth part of his kingdom to St Andrew in honour of God and the Virgin Mary.

The following night, while Óengus was asleep, St Andrew appears to him. He tells him that he himself has pleaded the cause of the Picts with Almighty God. God, says St Andrew, always answers the request of those who pray with sincerity and humility. Óengus can be confident of victory the next day, because he and many of his soldiers would see an angel holding the Cross of Christ at the head of his army as they broke free from the encircling Anglian force. But Óengus will only conquer if he gives God a tenth of his wealth immediately after the battle.

Bower adds that St Andrew reminds Óengus that his vow was made without any physical or psychological compulsion, but with the fully conscious use of his free-will. The indisputable meaning of this theological footnote is that Óengus would not on any legal grounds later be justified in dismissing his promise as having been made under duress and therefore not being binding.

If he were to renege on this solemn vow, he would be guilty of grave sin. In St Andrew's mind – in that of Walter Bower as he addresses the temporal leaders of his day – there must have been the strong likelihood that Óengus would be tempted not to fulfil his part of the bargain.

However, like Constantine before him, Óengus enters into a transaction with God, whose reward is physical survival but whose price is a tenth of his worldly goods.

When Óengus wakes, he describes everything in his dream to his generals and soldiers. Immediately their morale rises dramatically. They are changed men, fired up with unprecedented courage and aggression. The Picts attack, although outnumbered, screaming and blaring trumpets to startle and disorient their enemies.

The Angles are terrified. They break ranks and desperately begin to retreat. Only the king and his immediate bodyguard stand firm.

In a short space of time even they are surrounded and put to the sword. Athelstan's head is severed from his body and, by order of Óengus, placed in a prominent position on the island of Inchgarvie, visible to everyone crossing over the River Forth from Queensferry.

The account (based on the second version of the legend) given by Walter Bower of the display of Athelstan's severed head on a wooden pole at the island of Inchgarvie (a mere six kilometres southwest of Bower's own scriptorium – study – at Inchcolm and on one of the established pilgrim-routes to St Andrews), is suspiciously anachronistic. The crossing proper at Queensferry was only established in the reign of Queen Margaret (*circa* 1046-93).

If the (admittedly questionable) derivation by George Buchanan of 'Markle' as 'miracle' is correct as indicating the location of the vision of the Cross of Christ seen by the Picts, then it was seen to the east of the battle site. This would suggest that what the Picts saw in the sky was the early morning sun refracted against a blue summer sky rather than the cross of clouds of popular tradition.

In heraldic terms, the white Saltire cross (widely flown in Scotland and used in the badges of societies or industrial corporations) is only a representation of the colour silver. The early morning sun, silver in hue, convincingly fits this interpretation as to how the Scottish Saltire was first perceived.

As it was for Constantine at the Milvian Bridge, the *Chi Rho* became a mesmerising guarantee of victory while Óengus and his men began their offensive. The death of Athelstan is effected at the crossing-point over water. Like Maxentius, Athelstan has his head severed and displayed as a sign of triumph and as a warning.

But the overarching significance of the battle is the victory of the institutional Church and its symbiotic association with military and economic power. 'God is the ruler of all kings,' Andrew tells Óengus in his dream.

The story of the appearance of St Andrew to Óengus is repeated by most of the later Scottish historians – John Major (1469-1549); Hector Boece (*circa* 1470-1536); George Buchanan (1506-82); John Spottiswood (1565-1639) and John Leslie (1526-96).

Bower's version of the story is deftly compressed by the Reformer and Renaissance scholar, George Buchanan, in his *History of Scotland*, a twenty volume work completed shortly before his death. Buchanan also adds some details of his own:

During the night, after having set the watches, Óengus, who considered that without divine assistance all human efforts would be of little avail, devoted himself wholly to prayer, till, worn out with bodily fatigue and mental anxiety, he fell into a slumber, in which there appeared to him St Andrew, the Apostle, who promised him a glorious victory.

This vision being narrated to the Picts, flushed them with hope, and they prepared with alacrity for the conflict which they had now no means of escaping .... The next day being spent on skirmishing, they came on the third to a regular engagement.

It is added, that a decussated [intersecting at right-angles, derived from the Roman coin of *decem asses* – identified by the number X] *cross appeared in the sky, when they were about to engage, which so terrified the English that they were scarcely able to withstand the first attack of the Picts.*

According to the parish minister, Revd George Goldie, writing in the *First Statistical Account* (1791-99) and acknowledging his indebtedness to Buchanan's *Rerum scoticarium historia:* '... towards the end of the twelfth century, the parish churches of Athelstaneford and Crail in Fife, with their tithes, were annexed to the monastery of St Martin, in the parish of Haddington, by Malcolm IV.'

The *Second Statistical Account* (1845) seems to contradict Goldie:

History records that the lands on which the battle of Athelstaneford was fought and won, were given by the King of the Scots to the Culdee Priory of St Andrew, as an acknowledgement of gratitude to Heaven for the victory obtained. At the Reformation, when monkish institutions were abolished in Scotland, these lands were conferred on the Chapel Royal of

Holyroodhouse, with which they are still connected, and form a considerable part of the income drawn by the present dean or deans of that venerable fane. The late Sir David Kinloch, Baronet of Gilmerton, obtained from the Crown a perpetual lease of these lands.

Taken together, these two pieces of information appear to confirm that the battle-site passed into the ownership of the ecclesiastical authorities at St Andrews and they offer a convincing reason for the land being so assigned. In addition, we learn that the land was of considerable monetary value – presumably for farming.

The *Ordnance Survey Name Book* of 1853 contains the military surveyors' handwritten report of their mapping activities at Athelstaneford. One of their informants – a local farmer – told how he had been quarrying for stone some years previously and had unearthed a Christian long cist grave just to the southeast of the Cogtail Burn bridge.

The *Second Statistical Account* fills out the story:

In the cist was found the badly-decayed remains of a warrior, including part of the human cranium and the lower jaw. The coffin was but two and a half feet below the surface. It was formed of five handsome freestones – one at each side of the body, one at the head, another at the feet, placed at right angles, and one for covering. The stones forming the coffin had been cemented together with a fine paste made apparently of clay, to prevent the admission of the external air. A cavity had been cut in the surface of the hard rock, six feet two inches in length, thirty inches in breadth, and four in depth, in which the body had been laid, and where it was found.

This was believed to have been the body of the unfortunate Athelstan, who had apparently been in headlong flight when he was killed by an arrow. However, if Walter Bower is correct in saying that the head of the vanquished leader was displayed on an island in the Firth of Forth, then the skull in the Athelstaneford cist cannot be Athelstan's.

The Ordnance Survey map records the site of the battle on a wide, flat piece of ground to the north of Athelstaneford and to the west of the B1347, just south of the now-disused East Fortune airfield.

At one time there were two standing-stones: one at the southern limit of the battle site (near Athelmead), the other at the northern (near Greenburn). One stone has now been destroyed, the other removed.

While the Roman emperor Constantine's decision to accept the patronage of Christ made it possible for Church and State to be identified in a united christo-centric empire, Óengus' acceptance of Christ through his Apostle Andrew led to the foundation of a national shrine in a united kingdom centred on Christ through the relics of Andrew.

The *First Statistical Account*, enthused by George Buchanan's stately narrative, 'boasts proudly that it was Achaius, King of the Scots ... by whose assistance Hungus obtained this victory [for he sent him 10,000 men, under the command of his son Alpinus], in commemoration of the foresaid appearance of St Andrew's cross, he afterwards instituted an order of knighthood in honour of St Andrew'. In memory of the occasion, Kenneth II (971-95), King of Scots, instituted an Order of St Andrew.

Around the reign of Kenneth II, a version of the *Acts of Andrew* was written down in England. The 1700-line *Andreas,* written in Old English, was discovered in northern Italy in the archives of the Cathedral of Vercelli. Vercelli is on the main pilgrimage route to Rome and also has a thirteenth century church dedicated to St Andrew.

In the poem, the twelve Apostles are presented, in the style of the Viking epic, as warriors – 'glorious heroes'. Andrew is celebrated as a heroic missionary, sailing through violent storms (like the Greek St Regulus), who by his sufferings persuades others to receive the bath of baptism, abandon idolatry and destroy the old altars. With the aid of angels and through the power of God, Andrew receives supernatural help. He becomes invisible for a time in order to defeat his enemies. Although he is tortured near to death, his blood fertilises the earth, turning it, where it falls, into gardens of lush trees and fragrant flowers.

Andrew becomes not only a bringer of the Good News, but symbolises the fruitful nature of conversion and the tangible harvest which, according to the poet, will follow any nation's acceptance of the crucified Christ.

Chapter 6

The VOYAGE
of RULE

ACCORDING to the *Scotichronicon,* a Greek monk, Regulus
(anglicised as Rule), keeper of the Apostle Andrew's relics at
Patras, is warned by an unnamed angel to remove some of the saint's
bones from his sarcophagus in the shrine, hide them and wait for
further clarification. Two days later, the legions of the emperor Constantinus capture the city of Patras, strip it of all its wealth and
take the saint's relics away to Constantinople. (Regulus was perhaps
a symbolic figure of the Augustinian Canons Regular and their
'rule' of living. They were later responsible for editing and rewriting
the St Andrews foundation legend and for guarding the Apostle's
relics.)

The first version of the legend tells us that, following the battle of
Athelstaneford, the victors were in a quandary as to where to locate
the religious foundation which God had ordered them to establish.
In answer to their prayers, fasting and appeals to the mercy of God,
a monk named Regulus, one of the guardians of the body of the
Apostle Andrew not in Patras but at Constantinople, had a visionary
experience in which God revealed to him that, led by a guardian
angel, he must leave his own country, his way of life and his home,
and go to the land which God would show him – Mount Royal,
otherwise known as Kilrymont.

Walter Bower describes God's directive to Regulus quite differ-
ently: after a passage of several years, he writes, the same angel again
appears to St Rule and, with a fearsome expression on his face, tells
him to take the relics he has previously hidden and sail westwards to
the end of the world. Wherever he and his companions are almost
killed in a shipwreck, they are finally to end their journey and there
Rule is to lay the foundation of a church. And the angel foretells how,
just as people flocked to the East to hear Andrew preach while he was
alive, in future times pilgrims will come in great numbers to pray at

his new shrine in the West and be cured by the miraculous healing effected by the relics of the Apostle.

The second version of the story returns St Rule to Patras, but specifies the relics he has secreted as being three fingers of the right hand, an arm-bone from between the elbow and the shoulder, one kneecap, and a single tooth. The arm, of course, is part of the relic brought back from Constantinople by Pope Gregory, placed in his own monastery in Rome and partly transferred to England either by Augustine, Wilfrid or Acca. They are the same corporeal relics which formed the centre-piece of devotion and veneration in the great Cathedral of St Andrews. This detail of the story is therefore a confused version of the real events.

With a near-death experience, the foundation legend of Walter Bower (who knew so well the waters between East Lothian and Fife), comes to a dramatic climax. Lucky to be alive, shivering and bruised after a cataclysmic shipwreck, Rule and his companions, almost dead after their long (in one version, two-year) journey from Patras through the Mediterranean, up the west coast of Spain, Portugal and France and through the North Sea, manage to drag themselves ashore onto the coast of East Fife.

Then the truth dawns on them. It is 28 September, the feast of the Archangel Michael. (The second version of the story adds that their arrival takes place under cover of darkness). The implication of the legend is that the anonymous heavenly messenger who acted as intermediary between God and Rule, and who has guided them safely to their final destination, was none other than the Prince of Angels himself who led the victorious armies of the Lord.

Rule's first act is to place the Cross of Christ in a prominent position to protect them from the subversive effect of evil spirits. In Old Testament fashion he sets up tents for his missionaries and, leaving a number behind, goes on to Forteviot.

Although Rule is presumably a Greek monk, he evidently speaks Latin. At least we must assume that is how he manages to communicate with the local population, for at Forteviot he meets the three sons of King Óengus, who is in Argyll, and explains his mission. Rule travels north to meet Óengus near Braemar. On their return journey, Rule and Óengus dedicate churches, finally reaching Kilrymont (in Gaelic, *Cill Rimhinn* or *Cennrigmonaid*). There, Óengus makes a grant to Rule of thirty acres in Boar Wood (a grove of pigs or 'Muckross' in the language of the Picts; *cursus apri* in Latin), dedicated in the name of the Apostle Andrew to the greater glory of God.

St Rule displays the holy relics of the Apostle high above his head for all to see as he and his community process solemnly and sing psalms. Then the king and his earls walk in procession around Kirkhill where, in commemoration of the twelve Apostles and the twelve tribes of Israel, they erect and bless twelve stone crosses to mark the boundaries of holy ground.

There, in future years many incredible miracles are to occur from touching the relics – the blind see, the dumb speak, the lame walk, and healing is given by God to all those who ask for the Apostle's help.

From the year 787 it had been a requirement re-emphasised by the Seventh General Council of Nicea that every consecrated church should have a relic placed in its altar. However, a clear distinction had to be made between the devotion paid to the Virgin Mary and the saints, and the worship reserved for God.

Total worship (*latria*) was due to God alone; saints were to be venerated (*dulia*) and the Virgin Mary accorded an enhanced veneration as Mother of Christ (*hyperdulia*). In practice these distinctions were not always understood by the people, so giving rise to the abuses of exaggerated attention to the importance and power of the saints.

The saints were not to be venerated for themselves, but only in so far as their lives gave evidence of *grace,* the love and saving generosity of God. As outstanding examples of His Creation, they were believed to offer Christians an additional means of accessing the love of God. The lives of the saints were also a way of focusing prayer.

Time and again, the Latin of the manuscripts repeats the phrase '*Deo et Sancto Andreae*', emphasising that St Andrew is subordinate to Almighty God, to whom alone worship is to be given. The relics of Andrew are to be accorded veneration, but never *worship.*

The second version of the legend in addition distinguishes between the varieties of places of worship which Rule and Óengus set up. These are: *oratories* (small chapels); *ecclesias* (equivalent to a parish church) and *basilicas* (major churches or cathedrals).

The foundation legends for the shrine of the Apostle Andrew at Kilrymont do not correspond to what we would expect of historical records today. Nevertheless, running under the different versions of the legend, it is possible to pick out a number of strands of information which are likely to have a factual basis.

What is apparent is that the geographical movement of the bones of Andrew depended almost entirely on the initiatives of an emperor or king who was motivated principally by self-aggrandisement.

Conversely, there is nothing to connect the victorious battle at Athelstaneford to the arrival of the relics. They occur in different locations and on different occasions. They are parallel narratives and their time-scales do not coincide.

There are two separate but inter-linked parts in the legend: the battle of Athelstaneford and the arrival of St Rule. Both take place in the east of Scotland. The first takes place inland and south of the Firth of Forth; the second, at the coast and to the north of the Firth. This helps to impress the universal applicability of the legend to all Scots.

It is worth noting that there are other legends of the time which link the Lothians with Fife. The Apostle of Cumbria, St Kentigern (or Mungo) (*circa* 518-603) also provides a link between Lothian and Fife. His mother was said to have been the daughter of Loth, King of the Lothians. At his fort on Traprain Law (only a few miles from Athelstaneford), Mungo's mother, Princess Thenew, was thrown off the steep southern side of Traprain Law for becoming pregnant by a shepherd. She survived and managed to cross the Firth of Forth in a coracle to Culross in West Fife where her son, Mungo, was born.

At this point, Bower emphasises for his reader that Andrew will be a sure foundation for the Kingdom of Scotland, based on the solid rock of faith provided by Peter's brother, supported strongly in return by all the kings and estates of Scotland, centred on what would become the see of St Andrews. It is all very much in the spirit of Martin Luther's hymn *Ein feste burg* – in Thomas Carlyle's translation: 'A safe stronghold our God is still, A trusty shield and weapon.' Spiritual strength will be reciprocated by temporal prosperity. It is a spirituality of Covenant between God and his chosen people: in this case, the Scots.

Rule (like Gregory journeying to Constantinople accompanied by his fellow-monks from his monastery of St Andrew; or St Augustine setting off for England with his companions from the same monastery of St Andrew in Rome) gathers about him men and women of good life to make the momentous journey: St Damian, priest; Gelasius and Chubaculus, deacons; Merniacus the brother of St Damian; Nerius and Elrisenius from Crete; Mirenus, Machabeus, and Silvius his brother. There were also eight hermits – Felix, Sajanus, Matheus, Mauricius, Madianus, Philip, Luke and Eugenius – and three virgin saints from Colsoia –Triduana, Potencia and Emerea.

After a voyage of nearly two years, sailing without charts or knowing where their final destination was – beyond the Pillars of Hercules (between Spain and North Africa), Rule's ship is finally caught up by a powerful wind and smashed on the rocks in the kingdom of the Picts.

The themes of travelling and the sea is an important one in the life of Andrew the Apostle, intrepid voyager and fisher of men. This is, for Scots, one of Andrew's qualities with which they could readily identify.

It is significant that while Andrew preached and was crucified on the seashore at Patras, his shrine in Scotland was erected equally close to the sea.

Óengus, King of the Picts around the year AD 800, gave a tenth of his kingdom to St Andrew in return for the miraculous help he had been given in his expedition against the Saxons. Thirty-two years after his arrival in Fife, St Rule dies.

Both versions of the foundation story seem to have been drawn from related, if not identical sources. St Rule (French *Rieul*) is thought to be a confusion with St Regulus of Senlis. There was a church of St Andrew at Senlis and he was said to have come from Greece to Gaul in the fourth century.

Late medieval calendars celebrate the Scottish Regulus on the day of St Regulus of Senlis (30 March) and also on that of the Irish St Riaguil of Mucc-Inis (corresponding to 'Muckross' – the promontory of the pigs) in Lochderg (16 October) who was active at Kilrymont around AD 580. It may be that Regulus, the bringer of St Andrew's relics to Scotland, was a fiction, but the fiction could have been grafted onto an existing local cult.

It can be seen that in the legend of the battle of Athelstaneford and in that of St Rule, the master-architect who controls the development and outcome of the story is God. Both Óengus and Rule are totally free agents, but do not have the ability to shape their future without the divine intervention of St Andrew or the angel – both of whom are merely agents of a supreme God.

Like Constantine, Óengus faces almost certain defeat and death; St Rule also sails from Patras in fear of his life, only doing so because the angel – and the prospect of damnation for disobeying a heavenly command – makes him an offer he cannot refuse.

If Rule's pioneering voyage is carefully grafted into an Irish saint called Riaguil or a French saint Rieul, he also has two other functions. He disguises the unpalatable (to Scots) fact that the relics of Andrew came through the intermediary of English missionaries and he acts as a compressed semi-factionalised version of true events.

It should be emphasised neither Regulus nor Acca were the first to make a Christian foundation at Kilrymont. There was a monastery before 'Regulus' landed or Acca left Hexham. In 747 the Irish annals of Tigernach record the death of Tuathalain, Abbot of Cennrigmonaid (Scots:'Kilrymont'/'Kinrymont', literally 'Head of the King's mount').

Legend also relates that at Kilrymont there stood an ancient sacred grove of oak trees. It is said that when Christianity came to the site, in accordance with the policy of Pope Gregory, the Great Tree was carefully dismembered and parts of it incorporated into the rafters of the first Christian church. Later the oak tree came to take its place on the medieval city seals of St Andrews.

In the foundation legend, there are echoes of true events in that, for example, the mission of Rule and his voyage into unknown territory echoes that of Augustine by sea from Rome to Marseilles and then from northern Gaul to Kent. Similarly, the battle of Athelstaneford perhaps also echoes the defeat of Ecgfrith and the Northumbrian forces by Brude, King of the Picts in the battle of Nechtansmere (20 May 685) at Dunnichen near Forfar.

When attempting to date the arrival of Rule at Kilrymont, there are many chronological inconsistencies. It seems to be, for example, inaccurate chronology that allows Prince Nechtan to be attracted by the beauty of St Rule's fellow-voyager from Patras, the consecrated virgin Triduana, who disposes of the prince's unwanted attentions by sending him her beautiful eyes on a skewer.

Triduana, from her convent at Roscobie in Angus was to finish the rest of her days at Restalrig, near Edinburgh where a holy well dedicated in her name offered cures to those with diseases of the eye.

Being too complex, the ramifications of the true story of how the body of Andrew came to Patras, to Constantinople, to Rome, to Hexham, have been compressed by Bower and his fellow-Augustinian predecessors into a striking legend. This legend preserves an important kernel of truth – the Church of the Picts (and subsequently of the Scots) had authentic roots in the teaching of Christ and his Apostles.

THE BATTLE OF NECTANSMERE (DETAIL FROM THE ABERLEMNO STONE)

Chapter 7

ANDREW
THE SAINT

A S numerous references in papal correspondence testify, the major
pilgrimage centres in the world were Jerusalem, Rome, and
Compostela in Spain. The only centres outside the fringes of the
Mediterranean which could claim to possess major authenticated
corporeal relics of an Apostle were the shrines of St James in Compostela, of St Matthias in Trier, Germany, and of St Andrew in Fife.

The Dark Ages were rife with foundation-legends. Rival places of
pilgrimage struggled to outdo each other as economic considerations
took priority over the egalitarian vision of the Communion of Saints.
Local pride and imagination often attributed spurious antiquity to a
shrine or alleged its foundation by New Testament figures in order to
increase status and boost tourism.

A church in Marseilles, for example, was said to have been
founded by Lazarus and his sisters; another in Mantua by Longinus,
the soldier who pierced Christ's side on Calvary. Glastonbury claimed
Joseph of Arimathea as its founder. In Paris it was Dionysius the
Areopagite.

The case at St Andrews, however, was significantly different. There,
no attempt was made to attribute its foundation to a known person-
age from the pages of the New Testament. Moreover, the supposed
founder, Regulus (a Greek monk with a Latin name), functions as
storyteller's shorthand. He is the convincing and dramatic adhesive
which papers over the cracks in a truncated version of real events.

Early in its life, the shrine of the Apostle at Kilrymont was able
to attract widespread aristocratic respect. The Prophecy of Berchan
(which was an eleventh century poem) tells of several kings and
princes ending their days as pilgrims or religious in 'the home of the
Apostle at the boundary of the breakers'. King Constantine II of
Alba, son of Aed, retired to the monastic life at St Andrews in 940,
where he died as its abbot five years later. His son, Indulf, passed

43

away 'in the house of the same holy Apostle' ten years later. Another Aed, son of Maelmithid, an Irish royal prince, is recorded as having died at St Andrews in 965 while on pilgrimage

The foundation legends describe how, in addition to the main basilica dedicated to St Andrew, seven other chapels were built on the headland above the harbour. These would have been small buildings, perhaps made mainly of wood.

The original monastic foundation which existed when the relics of Andrew came to Kilrymont would have been Celtic, the fruit of many missionary initiatives from Ireland. The Celtic monks, follow-ing a rule and largely concerned with their own community's life of prayer, would be succeeded in later centuries by the Culdees (known in the time of James IV as 'Irish monks'). They co-existed, sometimes uneasily, as stubbornly divergent religious communities within the mainstream ecclesiastical structure.

The Culdees had begun as an eighth century reforming movement of Irish monks. Their strict rule of living encouraged strict observance of the sabbath and forbade the use of alcohol or music. Their sacred literature, illuminated manuscripts and work in precious metals, how-ever, were exquisitely imaginative and colourful.

At *Cill Rimhinn* (Kilrymont) the Culdees were a community which also served the religious needs of local people. In later centuries they would become hereditary priests, living a largely secular life which appears to have permitted them to marry. A Culdee community was probably established in St Andrews by around the year 950.

In the tenth century, a frequent pilgrim to the shrine of Andrew was St Godric of Finchale, who referred to it as 'the far-famed house of St Andrew'. For his contemporary, the author of the life of St Cadoc, it seemed reasonable for St Cadoc to round off pilgrimages to Jerusalem and Rome with a visit to the basilica of the Apostle Andrew.

Evidence of the growing importance of the shrine is to be found in a magnificent Pictish sandstone sarcophagus dating from the ninth century which was unearthed on the site in 1833. Framed between interlaced Celtic ornamentation, the central figure is that of David pulling apart the jaws of the lion, while armed men hunt rabbits and deer through a wood (perhaps Swine Wood – Muckross, or in Latin *cursus apri*).

The church now known as 'St Rule's' was constructed around 1070. It was designed as a reliquary church whose square tower (over 30 metres in height) would perform much the same function as the

Statue of Liberty in New York – a guide and landmark for pilgrims approaching by land or sea.

But by 1124 it became clear to King Alexander I that, in addition to a need to construct a larger and more appropriate church, something would have to be done to set the staffing of the the shrine on a more secure basis – there was no resident priest of the secular clergy and the shrine was served only by a handful of the increasingly irregular Culdees who by this time celebrated mass according to rites no longer in use but still claimed a hereditary share of church revenue. Regular weekly services or services on special occasions were not available to monarch or people.

Alexander, only a few months before his death in 1124, arranged for Robert, prior of his Augustinian community at Scone, to be elected bishop at St Andrews. It was not until twenty years later, after many legal and practical difficulties, that Bishop Robert, with the support of King David, was finally able to endow a priory of Augustinian canons at St Andrews which would become the most important church corporation in Scotland.

From the time of David I, royal ordinance decreed that those on pilgrimage should enjoy the King's Peace, a forerunner of the modern passport:

> *Those men that are on pilgrimage and are visiting holy places for their souls' health, shall have our firm peace in going and coming, so that no man does them wrong provided they behave lawfully.'* [Royal protection was also extended in the case of those in trouble with the law: *'If a man is away on pilgrimage to Jerusalem, St James or Rome, an accusation against him should be suspended until his return.*]

The Laws of the Burghs echoed this ruling:

> *If any man from the King's burgh go on pilgrimage with permission of the Church and his neighbours, to the Holy Land or to St James or to any other holy place for the health of his soul, his house and his household shall be in our Lord the King's peace and in the baillies' until God bring him home again.*

For pilgrims venturing abroad, there were fixed limits on the duration of their absence: England (three weeks); Paris, St Denis (seven weeks); Rome and St James (16 weeks); Jerusalem (one year).

Among the notable Scots who went on pilgrimage abroad was the fourteenth century soldier, Alexander Lyndesy, described as *justiciar* north of the Forth. He died on the island of Candia while on his way to Jerusalem. Normally permission to go on pilgrimage had to be obtained from the king. In December 1499, for example, leave was granted to Robert, Lord Lyle to go on pilgrimage. Nine years later, Patrick, Lord Lindsay of Kirkforther was given royal protection for his pilgrimage.

A colourful (perhaps exaggerated) description of a typical Scottish pilgrim is preserved in a late twelfth century chronicle connected with the Abbey of Bury St Edmunds. Abbot Sampson of Bury, records the chronicle, decided he had to go to Rome to ensure a suitable appointment to the now vacant church at Woolpit.

Because it was the time of the schism between Pope Alexander III and Pope Octavian (1159-64), the Abbot was terrified of being imprisoned in Italy, mutilated or tortured by the opponents of the Pope. He decided to go in disguise as a Scots pilgrim.

He dressed as a tramp, with ragged clothes, leggings and breeches and carried a pair of old shoes over his shoulders. He would shake his walking-staff violently at people who made fun of him, using threatening language 'after the manner of the Scots'. In his little wallet he carried a small jug for drinking.

In spite of all these precautions, Abbot Sampson was robbed just outside Rome. He lost all his money and was only able to return to England by begging from door to door.

By the eleventh and twelfth centuries, pilgrimages to St Andrews were sufficiently frequent and substantial to warrant the setting-up of two ferries across the Firth of Forth, supported by hostels on both shores. Within the shrine community itself, a hostel now existed which could cater for six guests at a time.

There were two main routes to St Andrews. Founded in the middle of the twelfth century by Duncan, fourth earl of Fife (and granted by his sons and heirs to the nuns of North Berwick), the longer ferry crossing from North Berwick (on the south bank of the Firth of Forth) to Ardross in Fife was known as the Earl's Ferry. It was supported by hostels in both ports. For bona fide pilgrims, passage on the ferry was free. A thirteenth century stone mould for making pilgrim's signs was unearthed in North Berwick last century. Its design shows St Andrew on his cross.

Further west was the older and better-known Queen's Ferry. It had been founded by Queen Margaret and also provided hostels at either shore. Later monarchs – David I, Malcolm IV, William the Lion, and Alexander II, all upheld the right of pilgrims to use the ferries free of charge. In the thirteenth century the crossing was re-founded by Bishop Malvoisin beside the bridge of Lochleven.

When pilgrims reached the northern shore, they would travel through Cupar by the king's highway to St Andrews. Pilgrims coming from the northeast of Scotland would cross the Firth of Tay from Taum in the ferry-boat, managed by the priory of St Andrews.

The bridge over the River Eden at Guardbridge just outside St Andrews was a *statio* (halting-place and assembly-point) on the pilgrimage road. By 1419, when Bishop Henry Wardlaw began to build the stone structure which can still be seen today, the eleventh century wooden bridge having been recently swept away in a flash-flood which had drowned a group of priests on pilgrimage.

In the 1150s, in preparation for the construction of the new cathedral church, Bishop Robert had his townplanners and engineers lay out four wide streets which converged towards the ecclesiastical centre of the town at the east. Medieval St Andrews seemed specifically planned to provide a circular route for a grand procession (North and South Streets), leaving Market Street, the centre, free for booths and stalls, where later merchants and itinerant showmen provided food, trade and entertainment. It might almost seem as if St Andrews is laid out according to the design of a pilgrim's scallop-shell – radiating streets converging into the shrine.

★ ★ ★

Under Robert's successor, Bishop Arnold, foundation work on the future cathedral church began in 1160 to the northwest of 'St Rule's'. In 1199 Pope Innocent III granted a licence to the Bishop of St Andrews to build a new church to meet the increase of the population in the parish of St Andrews.

As the building slowly progressed so did a new story of the travels of the bones of St Andrew shift from Scotland to Italy, to the Gulf of Salerno, and the picturesque coastal town of Amalfi some 62 kilometres south of Naples.

An independent republic from the 7th century until 1075, Amalfi was an important port and later became one of the principal Norman outposts. Amalfi had had ease of communication with the East from earliest times: Gregory the Great, writing in 596, makes earliest reference to the Christian community at Amalfi which acquired its first bishop that year and which became an archbishopric in 987. In later years, the Archdiocese of Amalfi became directly dependent on the Holy See.

Until 839 Amalfi had belonged to the Byzantine duchy of Naples. After that date, the city and its territory became an independent state within the orbit of the Byzantine Empire. From the ninth century, many Amalfitans were active in Mediterranean trade. Between 1055-1062 Amalfi tried in vain to organise an alliance of the West and East empires against the Norman invaders of southern Italy.

Amalfi's traffic with the East could be seen in its architecture. The magnificent doors of the Duomo (cathedral) Sant' Andrea, for example, had been commissioned by the head of the Amalfi colony in Constantinople and made there in 1066 before being shipped to Italy.

Onto the scene now strides Amalfi-born papal legate, Bishop Peter Capuano, who, while on a mission to Palestine, had learned of the capture and sack of Constantinople by the French Crusaders and quickly joined them in the city. There, in the church of Hagia Sophia, at a conference with clergy of the Greek rite in December 1204, he demanded that the Greeks conform to Roman liturgical practices.

Capuano, aware of the importance of the vast quantity of religious objects in Constantinople, set about gathering together many of the relics of the saints – the bodies of Andrew (from the Church of the Holy Apostles), Cosmas and Damian, Vitus and the hermit Macarius. In March 1206, Capuano, guarding the relics, arrived with a fleet of nine galleys at the port of Gaeta to the north of Naples and proceeded to transfer them to Amalfi.

Two years later, through the night of 7 May 1208, the body of the Apostle was given a place of honour in the city, with candles and incense burning, venerated by large numbers of the people.

At daybreak, the sun shone over Amalfi. The city had been newly decorated, hung with coloured cloths and sprinkled with flowers. A great crowd of people, singing hymns and carrying candles, went to meet the body.

The bishops, the Archbishop of Amalfi and the (by this time) Cardinal Capuano came forward barefoot to lift the coffin of St Andrew onto their shoulders. Then they carried it solemnly into the Cathedral, where the Cardinal preached to the people, asking them to honour the body of the Apostle by the worthiness of their lives. He opened the coffin of the Apostle, reverently showing the head and the other bones one at a time to the applauding crowd. The relics were immediately taken down into the crypt, placed in a silver container covered by a large slab of marble upon which the high altar was then constructed. The Apostle's bones were not to be seen again for many years.

In fact, the relics were divided into two portions and buried in two separate places, the skull being put in the least accessible location. Undoubtedly, the intention was to protect the relics from those who might wish to take the body back to Constantinople.

Eight years later, Pope Honorius III asked the Chapter (the canons or ruling body) of Amalfi Cathedral to release the relics of Andrew to Rome. The Chapter, however, refused to give up any part of the relics, saying that they did not know exactly where they had been hidden.

★ ★ ★

That year (1216) coincidentally is also the date of the papal bull of Honorius III which confirmed the constitutional basis of the Scottish Church – the *ecclesia scoticana*. This had already been established in 1192 by Pope Celestine III's Papal bull *Cum universi* which placed the Scottish church under the Holy See as a 'special daughter' (*filia specialis*) without any intermediate authority.

From as early as the twelfth century, the papacy had noted the particular loyalty of Scottish monarchs to the faith and to Rome. Members of the Scottish royal family such as Queen Margaret with her ecclesiastical reforms, or David I with his widespread introduction of new monastic orders into Scotland and his foundation of Scottish abbeys, made Scotland from a Roman perspective in many respects a model kingdom.

But, in spite of his missionary zeal, King David I failed to win the one concession from the papacy that would have meant more than all the rest – the conferring of archiepiscopal rank upon the ancient see of St Andrews.

Both York and Canterbury had attempted to exercise control over the Scottish Church, but it was not until the pontificate of Rolando Bandinelli (Pope Alexander III, 1159-81) that any substantial advance was made to protect the Scottish church from their predatory English neighbours.

Alexander's successor, Pope Lucius, gave Malcolm IV's brother, William the Lion, a mark of special favour – the Golden Rose. Pope Urban III (1185-7) also recognised the church (*ie* the diocese) of Glasgow as a 'special daughter' of Rome, without any intermediate authority. Celestine III (1191-8) extended this close dependence to the entire Scottish Church, except for the bishoprics of Galloway (which remained under the Archbishop of York) and the Isles and Orkney (under the Norwegian province of Trondheim).

As well as confirming Celestine III's *Cum universi*, Honorius III also gave Scots clergy the right to hold regular councils presided over by a specially appointed bishop. For Scotland, the papacy was the ultimate spiritual court of appeal and, when necessary, the court of first instance. On matters of great importance, special envoys (*legates*) would be sent to Scotland to conduct affairs on behalf of the papacy.

In the year 1250, the long-lost cross of St Andrew from Patras, was re-discovered at the monastery of St Victoire at Weaune near Marseilles. Legend had it that the cross was given by the Burgundians to the monastery in the first century AD. During the campaigns of Charles Martel against the Saracens in the eighth century, the cross had been lost. Most of the relic was destroyed finally in 1793, but some small portion was preserved intact. In 1980 this was handed over to the Cathedral at Patras.

Part of this relic, in a silver case, was taken by Philip, Duke of Burgundy to Brussels where, in 1429, he formed the Order of the Golden Fleece whose badge is the saltire or Cross of Burgundy. In 1477, the Burgundians came under the King of France. There were also connections between Burgundy and Scotland: in 1497 Pedro de Ayala, Spanish ambassador to Scotland, wrote to Ferdinand and Isabella of Spain that the Dukes of Burgundy wore the saltire of St Andrew in memory of help Scotland had once given Burgundy.

In the thirteenth and fourteenth centuries, Scotland was forced to defend itself against the ambitions of Edward I of England and his son Edward II. Edward I, claiming overlordship of Scotland, had had a seal made in 1291 with the figure of St Andrew upon it and it was political correctness of a very astute kind that arranged for Edward's choice as King of Scotland – John Balliol – to be inaugurated on St Andrew's Day, 1292.

But in this struggle to survive as an independent nation, Scotland received notable support from Pope Boniface VIII, who, in his letter *Scimus, fili* (1300), commanded Edward to end his incursions north of the Border. Scotland, asserted Boniface, belonged to the Holy See because it had been miraculously converted to the Christian faith by the relics of St Andrew. Tradition has it that when the Archbishop of Canterbury delivered the pope's letter to Edward at Sweetheart Abbey, he was almost too apprehensive to face the king.

In the very same year, the next episode in the story of the Apostle Andrew takes place in Amalfi. The less important parts of the body of the Apostle (not the skull), were unexpectedly found in the silver container under the high altar in which Cardinal Capuano had had them buried almost a century before. But it was not until three hundred years later that the other parts of the body (including the skull), were again discovered in the same church.

THE GREAT PILGRIM ASSEMBLY STATION AT GUARDBRIDGE 1438 –
STATIO PRINCIPALIS GAVEBRIGENSIS
(BY JUREK PÜTTER DA)

Chapter 8

RELICS
AND POLITICS

IN Scotland, meanwhile, it was not until 5 July 1318 that the consecration of the new St Andrews Cathedral took place. Probably the actual *rituale* (order of service) used at the consecration was the Pontifical of Bishop David Bernham – now in the Bibliothèque Nationale, Paris – which had been used during the thirteenth century by the bishops of St Andrews, David Bernham and William Wishart.

In the presence of seven bishops, 15 abbots and almost all the nobility of Scotland, King Robert the Bruce, representing the people of Scotland, interrupted the traditional format of the consecration by announcing an unprecedented annual endowment of one hundred merks sterling to the upkeep of the cathedral as a thanksgiving for the victory at Bannockburn four years before.

This consecration of a church in gratitude for victory in war is a virtually unique gesture in medieval Europe. The King went on to divide the spoils of Bannockburn among the churches of Scotland. Among other trophies, St Andrews Cathedral received a cross of rock crystal, and it is probable that the two statues of the Virgin Mary and St Andrew were placed in the church by the Douglas family about the same time.

With a total interior area of 2415 square metres and an interior length of 108 metres, the new cathedral was the visible evidence of a new national Church. The interior length of its nave was smaller than Canterbury Cathedral (157 metres), York (148 metres), Durham (121 metres), or the medieval basilica of St Peter, Rome (400). However, it was larger than that of Aeneas Sylvius Piccolomini's home cathedral of Siena (97 metres), larger than Amalfi (57 metres), Glasgow (86 metres), and even Santiago de Compostela (96 metres).

The national Church's credibility rested on the few small pieces of bone which were believed to be the body of the Apostle. As the

52

Marquess of Bute was to remark many centuries later (1894) when delivering his rectorial address at St Andrews University:

> *Whatever the history of these bits of bone, and whether they were or were not part of the body of the first-called Apostle of Christ, they were undoubtedly believed at the time to be genuine, and they were the immediate cause of the creation of St Andrews as the great national church of Scotland.*

And it was a sumptuous interior that visitors walking across the orange terracotta tiles of the Cathedral nave could see. The brightly coloured statues were covered with valuable offerings. North and south of the high altar were the principal images of the Virgin Mary and St Andrew whose votive lamp was maintained by the Douglas family. On feast-days, a huge red carpet covered the floor of the sanctuary.

On the altar were velvet cushion book rests; silver-gilt cruets held the water and wine, and holy water would be scattered using a silver *aspersarium*. Behind the altar, there was (certainly from the mid-fifteenth century) a painted triptych. This would very probably have rivalled in quality the Trinity Altarpiece (with its panel depicting James III protected by St Andrew) commissioned for the charitable foundation of Trinity College, Edinburgh by Edward Bonkil, from the Ghent artist, Hugo van der Goes (*died* 1482).

Few pilgrims would penetrate into the innermost Chapel of the Relics where the remains of St Andrew were enshrined. It stood beyond the screening *reredos* of the high altar.

The reliquary containing the bones of St Andrew was housed in a *relict aumbry* (shrine) in the centre of the chapel, built high enough to be seen over the reredos of the high altar by the choir.

In front of the *relict aumbry* was an altar. Around the walls were the other aumbries which held relics and other treasures of the church. Security was a major consideration. No medieval inventory of the relics and treasures survives, but we do know that in addition to the ancient reliquary containing the bones of Andrew, there were other jewels such as the silver shaft of King Alexander I (*circa* 1077-1124) which had been made into a processional cross. There were also 40 centimetre long tusks of ancient boars from the Boar's Raik. These were fixed by small chains to the choir stalls. Another treasure was the crystal cross taken from the field of Bannockburn.

The bones of St Andrew were not enshrined in separate reliquaries, but were all preserved in one reliquary. This is remarked upon by the

English chronicler, John Hardyng, who visited St Andrews in the early fifteenth century.

The reliquary would have been made by craftsman of the Celtic era, and like other reliquaries of that period it had a traditional Celtic name.

Just as the the crosier-reliquary of St Fillan, for example, was called the 'Quigrich', and the enshrined psalter of St Columba known as the 'Cathach', so the reliquary of St Andrew was 'Morbrac' (the Great Reliquary), from the Gaelic *breac* meaning 'bright', from its multi-coloured enamelling and the gold and silver of its decoration.

At the beginning of the thirteenth century, the name 'Morbrac' is to be found in an agreement drawn up over the lands of Scoonie and Garriach, in which a certain Gellin, son of Gillecrist Maccusseger, is guaranteed by the canons of St Andrews that he will have the privilege of carrying the Morbrac, just as Gillemur his predecessor formerly did, and will have the emoluments of food and clothing which his predecessor had enjoyed.

The principal public appearances of the Morbrac were when it was carried in solemn procession through the city. We have no information about these processions. There would be one on the principal feast of St Andrew – Andermass, the 30 November. But Walter Bower tells us that there was also one on 6 February when the feast of the Translation (arrival) of the relics was celebrated.

In preparation for the procession, the streets of the town would be cleaned at public expense. The trade guilds would provide religious tableaux or pageants to walk in the procession. The masters and scholars of the colleges would carry flowers and leafy branches. The Blackfriars and the Greyfriars would take part, as would the Culdee canons of the Chapel Royal of St Mary of the Rock.

The Augustinian canons of the metropolitan church would take pride of place near the reliquary. They would wear the finest vestments from the cathedral sacristy and wear garlands of flowers or jewelled bands around their heads.

Before the procession, the base would be placed during solemn High Mass in the middle of the chancel. The Morbrac in its housing would then be carried on its base mounted on a wooden stretcher under a canopy, either by the canons of the cathedral or by prominent laymen.

In the procession, hymns would be sung and the bells of the cathedral and other churches would ring out. Afterwards, after dusk, bonfires would be lit and fireworks set off into the night sky.

The *Scotichronicon* quotes an *ex voto* inscription which listed the nationalities who came to St Andrews – Franks, Normans, Flemings, Teutons, English, Germans, Dutch, French, Italians – many combining piety with trade.

The St Andrew-based historical illustrator, Jurek Pütter, sets the scene as the pilgrims arrived at the shrine of the Apostle:

The Morbrac is covered with a very large, comparatively unadorned black box in the shape of a house. When people were ushered in to the darkened reliquary chamber (a lot of these events were conducted in the evening) several small candles were lit, just enough to reveal the mysterious appearance of the black box. As more candles were lit you had the Augustinians beginning the first liturgical rites, solemn prayers, then the box would start to be raised. As it's raised, the cables holding the box have trips on them, so that as the cable rises up, it trips the bells. It's like a musical-box. What you had was the tremendous visual spectacle of an enormous black box being lifted up to reveal the glittering ornament of the reliquary underneath. Candles and oil lamps would be progressively lit whilst all this was going on. This is a standard device. The musical-box tripped bells so you had a melody being played as the box was lifted.

According to Pütter, the box (constructed to follow the house shape of the Morbrac) was lightly constructed so that it didn't impose a great weight. It could be cranked up and it was always cranked behind the screens so that the pilgrims didn't see the physical apparatus for hoisting. Again there was a sense of mystery. Yet the black box was always unadorned, for obvious reasons. It created a wonderful sense of mystery when a pilgrim entered the richly decorated reliquary chamber.

The one thing that stood out, in contrast, was the black box. It would have been an enormous thing. Maybe eight or nine feet long; six feet wide; maybe as much as six to seven feet high. When it was lifted, inside it would have been painted a dark blue with silver stars, so that, as it was being lifted, you could see a cosmos being revealed. It's still a device especially in Spain, Portugal, Italy even from the later Middle Ages and the Renaissance period. As musical instruments and mechanical devices improved, then you had great revivals in reliquary shrines as technology was used to further heighten the impact. The New World, Mexico, the whole of South America, where you have these devotional shrines, still have similar devices.

The reliquary chamber could maybe take 40 or 50 people at a time, but pilgrims were not permitted to enter into the shrine unattended and unsupervised. From time when thefts and public disorder were at their height, the Augustinians, who were the authorities in St Andrews, would only permit special guests to view the relics. But by and large, the average pilgrim did come into the reliquary chamber and was treated to this. It wasn't a spectacle that was available on demand. It was a controlled, arranged spectacle, simply because of theft, of damage, because of the danger of hysteria.

The average pilgrim did catch sight of the relics, but they were never permitted to touch them or get close to them. The only time the Morbrac was moved was on feast-days. Then its bier was slotted into the steps in front of the high altar slots which can still be seen today.

The effect of pilgrimage on the size of the local population could be dramatic, so all pilgrim cities had their population capped. Pilgrim cities were not permitted to grow beyond their capacity to sustain both their indigenous population and pilgrims.

While the emphasis was on pilgrims, not on the town's population, the authorities worked to an equation. There was no point advertising pilgrimages throughout the whole of Christian Europe if, at the end of the day, they couldn't be fed. Feeding people was more important than housing them, because in summer months you could still camp outside.

Jurek Pütter points out:

It was of paramount importance that people were fed, if they were an international pilgrim in residence for two to three months. Cities like Dunfermline were fixed at a population of about 2000; St Andrews to about 5000. It never grew – it was not permitted to grow.

Nick Haplin, today a Dundee University student counsellor, comments:

St Andrews was really a service city. Its most lucrative activity was the great bed-and-breakfast industry. It had the ability to accommodate additional thousands, especially at the high summer months of the year. That was how much of the city's wealth was generated.

To accommodate the pilgrims the *statios* were constructed. The pilgrim Statio at Guardbridge was between 60 to 90 metres across. Its dormitory could accommodate, at its last development, about 200 people. In the evenings the refectory was converted to a dormitory. In the summer months the pilgrims actually stayed encamped in the courtyard. Earlshall Castle nearby was probably largely constructed for Sir William Bruce in 1546 using stone taken from the demolished Statio. And when Sir Robert Lorimer came to restore the castle in the late nineteenth century, he designed a stone gateway in the garden which is surmounted by the ancient pilgrims' badge, the scallop shell, as if to remind the casual visitor of St Andrews' long association with pilgrimage.

The real value of a pilgrimage was the journey. King Edward I of England had a particular interest in pilgrimages. In 1270, two years before he became king, he had established a fine reputation as a knight on the Eighth (and last) Crusade.

Three years later, safe-passage to go on pilgrimage to St Andrews was granted on behalf of King Edward (who did not return to England for his coronation till 1274), to three Englishmen: Richard, son of Philip, Lawrence Scot, and Nicholas de Wygenhale.

But the most detailed account of an ordinary pilgrim's visit to St Andrews, and his motivation for it, is to be found in the case of William Bondolf, a cleric and burger of Dunkirk (possibly an Englishman), who had murdered Andrieu d'Esquerdes (perhaps a Scot named Andrew Ker – from the Scots word for 'left', corrie). Bondolf was ordered to pay a fine of 12 livres, to have 13 masses sung for the soul of the deceased and to make the pilgrimage to St Andrews – presumably because the victim was Scottish. On 29 May 1333, Bondolf completed his pilgrimage and received a certificate and seal of authentication from the prior of St Andrews, John of Gowrie. On 26 June 1333, Bondolf was back in France at Saint-Omer, where he presented his certificate and received absolution from his crime.

St Andrew could also be invoked for protection from disease. The English chronicler Thomas Walsingham (died circa 1422) records a prayer Scots used in 1379, which asked God and St Andrew to shield them from the pestilence, 'the foul death that Englishmen dien upon.'

November 30th was also significant in battle. During Scotland's second civil war, the turning-point came on St Andrew's Day 1335 when one of Balliol's supporters, David of Strathbogie, was defeated and killed by Andrew Murray.

A red letter day came on 3 February 1414 when St Andrews

University was founded. In the procession on 6 February, to mark this momentous event some 400 clerics joined with a host of layfolk.

In the late autumn of 1435, however, fate stepped once more into the developing mystery of the relics of St Andrew.

The Italian scholar and diplomat, Aeneas Silvius Piccolomini (then still a layman), was sent from France by Cardinal Nicholas Albergati to meet James I in order to persuade the king to launch an attack on England to help end the Hundred Years' War. A subsidiary aim of Piccolomini's secret mission was to restore the status of Scottish archdeacon William Croyser, who had been condemned for treason and deprived of his office in the papal courts at Florence.

Preparing to cross over to England in the autumn of 1435, Piccolomini was first arrested at Calais and then released. On his way to London to see his close friend, the Englishman Adam de Molin (*protonotario* – senior secretary to the Avignon papacy), Piccolomini visited the shrine of St Thomas à Becket in Canterbury. In his memoirs, written almost thirty years later from notes believed to have been made in his own diaries, Piccolomini speaks with awe of the golden mausoleum of Thomas which glittered with diamonds, pearls and carbuncles. On another occasion he was to speak with admiration of the stained glass windows in York Minster, which he saw, probably in 1436, on his journey back from Scotland.

To reach London, Piccolomini would have passed through Rochester with its shrine of St Andrew. But, in spite of the efforts of his friend Adam de Molin, Piccolomini was refused permission to travel overland to the Scottish Border. England, unlike Scotland and France, had remained loyal to the rival Roman pontiff.

Frustrated once more, Piccolomini returned to the Continent, going first to Bruges and then Sluys. From Sluys, he and his servants set sail for Scotland – perhaps aiming for St Andrews, the religious and administrative centre of the country in contrast to the court of James I, which periodically moved with the monarch between several locations.

Writing of himself as he was at that time, a cultivated diplomat of thirty, the sixty-year old Pius II tells his story in the third person:

> *Then he took ship for Scotland, but was driven to Norway by two violent gales, one of which kept them in fear of death for 14 hours.*

He describes himself and his sailing-companions as being totally disoriented and at the mercy of the elements as they headed towards what he believed was a deprived and culturally barren nation:

The other gale pounded the ship for two nights and a day, so that she sprang a leak and was carried so far out to sea toward the north that the sailors, who could no longer read the constellations, abandoned all hope.

Piccolomini turns his adventures into a parable with a moral:

But the Divine mercy came to their aid, raising north winds, which drove the vessel back toward the mainland and finally on the twelfth day brought them in sight of Scotland.

The ship, still taking in water, manages to limp into port:

When they had made harbour [probably at Belhaven Sands, west of Dunbar], *Aeneas, in fulfilment of a vow, walked barefoot to the nearest shrine.*

To get to the nearest shrine (fragments of which have recently been discovered), Aeneas would have to cross the Peffer Burn which, as the Cogtail Burn, runs all the way from Athelstaneford. Since he walked five miles to 'the holy well at Whitekirk dedicated to the Virgin Mary', it can be assumed that his ship did not land close to Dunbar (which had a sizeable collegiate church). Even after the Reformation, the custom of 'creeping' to Whitekirk continued.

After resting there for two hours, he found on rising that he could not walk a step, his feet were so weak and numb with the cold. It was his salvation that there was nothing there to eat and he had to go on to another village.

It is possible that the second village he visited was North Berwick:

While he was being carried there by his servants, Aeneas warmed up his feet by continuously banging them on the ground. Against all expectation, he recovered and was able to walk again.

As a result of this mortification, Piccolomini was to suffer from rheumatism for the rest of his life.

Being based on notes in his diary written many years before, Piccolomini's account is selective and cannot always be entirely trusted – it was written when he would have have his dignity as pope to consider. He implies that he fulfilled his mission (of which he says nothing), in that he met the king – where, we are not told (in Edinburgh or perhaps Perth) – and spent some seven months in Scotland.

In the Piccolomini Library in Aeneas's home town of Siena, the painter Pinturicchio's imaginative fresco of 1505-8, with its chinoiserie interpretation of the Scottish landscape, does little to shed light on the events of his visit to Scotland. However, it is tempting to see, in the coastal city far behind the king's head, a representation of St Andrews with its fortified walls, towers and steeples.

Piccolomini was not able to arouse James against England as he had hoped. The Scots king proved himself immovable, in spite of all Aeneas' attempts to persuade him otherwise. Perhaps this explains Aeneas' uncharacteristic description of the Scots king in his *Commentaries* as being squat and thick-set. James, a patron of the arts and author of the collection of poems known as *The Kingis Quair*, had been a prisoner of the English for 18 years. He had been educated in England and, having a fine physique, even fought for Henry V in France. During his reign in Scotland, James placed considerable importance on finance and law and order. In his relations with the Church, however, he was abrasive. This may partly explain his assassination, two years after Aeneas' visit, at the Dominican friary in Perth.

James' response to Aeneas was to refuse to declare war on England, although he did promise not to provide assistance to the English. Although James did not reinstate archdeacon William Croyser, he observed the niceties of diplomacy by reimbursing Aeneas for his travelling expenses and giving him money and two horses for his return journey through England.

Writing in April 1436 to his patron, Cardinal Albergati, Aeneas excuses himself for not having communicated with him during the seven long and painful months he had endured the Scottish climate and culture. He indicates that Scotland was economically and culturally deprived, that he had no means of getting a private letter out of the country, and adds that in any case no developments took place during his stay which could remotely affect Albergati's political concerns. Scotland, according to Piccolomini's official report, was of little importance.

However, in his later account of Scotland contained in his *Commentaries* and the brief geographical notes in his *Europa,* Aeneas gives a version of his Scottish mission which is quite the reverse to this tight-lipped, damage-limitation correspondence which attempts to gloss over the failure of his mission. His hidden agenda as an ambitious young man was to persuade Albergati of the hardships he had had to endure in Scotland in faithfully carrying out his master's instructions.

In his *Commentaries,* in contrast, Aeneas the Renaissance humanist is at pains to paint a bizarre, arresting picture of the idiosyncrasies of a cold and far-off nation which burned black stones for fuel and was said to have geese growing on trees. Here he makes use of the tradition of travel-writing popularised by the fourteenth century *Voyage of Sir John Mandeville,* a guide for pilgrims to the Holy Land which combined geography, natural history, romance and marvels.

Nine years later, in a letter to his father, Piccolomini reveals yet another motive for masking his real experiences north of the Border and for his seven months stay in the country: he had fathered a son by a Scots woman, but the child died after a few years of life.

Knowing Aeneas' interest in the shrine at Canterbury, it is unthinkable that, during his time in Scotland, he would not have crossed to Fife and on to the metropolitan Cathedral at St Andrews where, as a high-ranking but covert ecclesiastical emissary, he would have paid his respects to Bishop Henry Wardlaw. However, despite the high probability of a visit to the shrine of the Apostle, Aeneas is intriguingly silent about the relics at St Andrews.

True to his name, Aeneas' experiences in Scotland also reflect to some extent the wanderings of the Aeneas of Classical legend who, like him, endured exile, shipwreck and isolation. It is possible that the poet Gavin Douglas (*circa* 1474-1522), himself born at Tantallon Castle on the East Lothian shore two miles from Whitekirk, may have partly drawn upon Piccolomini's travels in his translation into Scots of Virgil's *Aeneid,*which he finished about 1513.

Douglas was educated at St Andrews University and later studied at Paris. In 1514 he appealed (unsuccessfully) to Pope Leo X to be appointed as Archbishop of St Andrews, but the following year was made Bishop of Dunkeld. His translation (1513) into Scots of Virgil's *Aeneid* vividly describes the shipwreck of the classical Aeneas, much as Aeneas Sylvius Piccolomini must have experienced it on the eastern coast of Scotland. And in his prologue to Book VII, Douglas captures the radical discomfort of the Scottish rural and urban winter which had so tormented Piccolomini nearly 80 years before:

Persavyt the mornyng bla, wan and har,
With clowdy gurn and rak ourquhelmyt the ayr …

The dew droppis congelit on stibbill and rynd,
And sharp hailstanys mortfundeit of kynd
Hoppand on thak and on the causay by.

Twenty years after his visit to Scotland, Piccolomini spent some time touring near Naples. He visited the tombs of Saints Andrew and Matthew. He went to Baiae and Cumae (where Aeneas had been taken by the Sibyl to the nether world and whose prophecies Maxentius had consulted before the battle of Milvian Bridge). Piccolomini also visited Salerno and then Amalfi with its relics of Andrew. He saw the reputed tomb of Virgil and all the places in the neighbourhood that had associations with the Classical era or which preserved actual relics of antiquity.

In 1458, Aeneas Silvius Piccolomini was elected Pope Pius II. Within two years the Turks, under Sultan Mehemet II, had invaded the Greek Peloponnesus. Anxious to preserve his own skin, Thomas Palaeologus, the Despot of Morea and brother to the last Christian emperor of Constantinople, seized the head of the Apostle Andrew from Patras and took it, together with his family, to Corfu, hoping to use the relic as a bargaining-counter to ensure his safety.

The Pope, on hearing that Palaeologus was likely to sell the head to the highest bidder, wrote to Thomas asking him to bring it to Rome, to be placed beside the bones of its brother St Peter. Pius promised to shelter both the head and the Despot as long as danger threatened, in the hope that Thomas and the head might one day might be restored.

Thomas Palaeologus landed at Ancona on the north-east coast of Italy on 16 November 1460, but did not arrive in Rome until 7 March the following year. The head of St Andrew, meanwhile, was deposited in the citadel of Narni until the Pope could master the civil conflict in and around Rome.

Finally, with his wife and four children, Palaeologus arrived in Rome during Lent of 1461. Pius was full of sympathy for the exile and gave him lodgings at San Spirito in Sassia (where Pius would later also deposit relics of the Apostle Andrew).

When peace was finally restored, Pius sent out proclamations to the chief cities of Italy promising indulgences, saying that the more people who were present in Rome, the more magnificent the head's welcome would be.

Pius had planned to bring out the heads of the Apostles Peter and Paul to greet the head of St Andrew, but they were so weighed down with lead and silver that they had to be left on view at the Lateran.

The approach to the basilica of St Peter was quickly upgraded to cope with the crowds who were to come to be inspired with belief in the eventual triumph of the Christians over the Turks. New steps were built and two colossal statues of the Saints Peter and Paul by Paolo Romano were erected on each side at the base of the steps.

The ceremony of St Andrew's head took place during Easter week 1462. Whole houses had been cleared away from the piazza of St Peter's and, inside the church, the tombs of medieval popes and cardinals in the middle of the nave were pushed to the sides of the building.

Near the Ponte Molle (the Milvian Bridge), to commemorate the ceremony of St Andrew's head, a marble tabernacle was erected on the spot where Pius would receive the relic along with a statue of St Andrew (again by Paolo Romano), thus confirming the symbolic link with Constantine.

Inside the basilica itself, a chapel was dedicated to St Andrew. It contained a tabernacle supporting a ciborium (container) with gilded marble reliefs of the Apostle's head by Paolo Romano and Isaia da Pisa. Inside was the silver-gilt reliquary by Simone da Firenze.

The platform from which Pius showed the Apostle's head to the assembled crowds was hung with tapestries for the occasion and was probably dismantled immediately after the ceremony, as the Pope left Rome in May 1462 and did not come back until December.

Six weeks before the ceremony, Pius called together his six most trusted cardinals and confided in them his deep concern about the Turkish successes which were threatening to overwhelm Christianity in the Levant. Pius was making an effort to win the support of the self-interested princes for the crusade through the startling public relations coup offered by the ceremony of St Andrew's head. He was using the ceremony to ask St Andrew's help through St Peter and St Paul so that, by defeating the Turks, it would be possible for the head to return in glory to Greece, for Thomas Palaeologus to return to power.

Close to the Ponte Molle, on the first day of the ceremony, Palm Sunday, 12 April 1462, Pius, very moved, received the head from a weeping Cardinal Bessarion (a Greek expatriate scholar and theologian, cardinal 1439-73 and titular Latin patriarch of Constantinople). A pen and ink drawing attributed to Ventura Salimbeni, now in the Museo Horne, Florence records the occasion.

After Pius' speech of welcome – and a short prayer that by the Apostle's intercession, the insolence of the faithless Turk might be crushed – the choir sang a hymn.

That night the head stayed at the church of Santa Maria del Popolo. There was a storm which made the superstitious Romans restive, but the next day was radiant in anticipation of the ceremony.

The front of the two-mile procession through the centre of Rome reached St Peter's before the Pope – carried in his golden chair and holding St Andrew's head sheltered from the sun by a golden *baldachino* (canopy) – could start from Santa Maria del Popolo.

St Peter's was already filled with a crowd of strangers and from them arose a noise of voices like the murmur of many waters, since at the sight of the Apostle's head 'all fell to beating their breasts and with groans and wailings commended themselves to it'.

Although it can be assumed that some foreigners were present – such as members of the papal administration – Piccolomini, in his description of the foreign dignitaries present, does not mention any from Scotland.

The inside of the basilica seemed one blaze of lights and there was the glow of innumerable lamps and candelabra, made still more marvellous by the music of the organ and the singing of the clergy.

The head of St Andrew was set down on the altar and Cardinal Bessarion, on behalf of St Andrew, addressed St Peter and then the Pope, urging him not to stop exhorting Christian princes to support the Crusade through which one day they would win everlasting fame. It was the supreme moment of Aeneas Sylvius Piccolomini's life.

On Easter Sunday, the Apostle's head was exhibited along with the veil of Veronica, the Volto Santo. At the end of the ceremonies, the head was deposited in the Castel' Sant' Angelo until a proper receptacle could be prepared for it. This was not done until the following year, when not only was a new reliquary made but also a tabernacle (tent-shaped box) on four supporting columns.

Pius, in a gesture commemorating Gregory the Great's acquisition of the relic of St Andrew in Constantinople, placed the reliquary over Gregory's tomb, which he had moved to his new chapel in the course of reorganising the basilica. The statue of St Andrew which later stood on St Gregory's tomb was placed there in 1570 by Pius' descendant, Francesco Bandini Piccolomini.

The white and gilded marble reliquary could not be missed by those who entered the church. Three marble reliefs by Isaia da Pisa and Paolo Romano taken from the lunettes of the reliquary, survive today in the Grotte Vaticane. The original Patras reliquary was later sent to Pienza when the new one (77 centimetres high) was made.

On 23 September 1463, at a secret consistory following the reception of St Andrew's head, the Pope urged the Church to return to abstinence, purity, innocence, zeal for the faith, religious fervour, scorn of death and eagerness of martyrdom, in preparation for the Crusade for which he would leave on 18 June 1464. 'We must,' urged Pius II, 'draw near to those earlier saints.'

The significance of the St Andrew chapel in the history of St Peter's is not small. It could be said it was the first time a Renaissance pope cleared a prominent place in the basilica not only for a specific saint, but for himself. Pius ordered that he should be buried in this chapel, thus once more identifying his cause with that of St Andrew – the Crusade against the Turks which led to Pius' eventual disappointment and death. Pius' lengthy description of the complex ceremonies offer some suggestion as to the spirit in which the Great Morbrac, with its reliquary of the Apostle, would be celebrated in St Andrews.

As for the Piccolominis, they continued to forge personal links with the major locations of the bones of St Andrew. Aeneas Sylvius' nephew Antonio was created Duke of Amalfi around 1463, while Alexander Piccolomini (later Pius III) was consecrated Archbishop of Patras a century later. In the time of Pius V, St Andrew's chapel in St Peter's was demolished and Pius III's tomb transferred to the church of Sant' Andrea della Valle.

Nine years later there were fresh ecclesiastical developments in Scotland. When Patrick Graham became its first archbishop in 1472, the see of St Andrews was elevated to the dignity of an archbishopric with Metropolitan status. A bull of Pope Sixtus IV (1414–84) raised Bishop Graham to the rank of archbishop and made all twelve Scottish bishoprics suffragans under the see of St Andrews.

An important decision in Rome was marked by the reissue of a bull of Clement III – that papal judges-delegate were to hear Scottish cases in Scotland or in Durham or Carlisle, but never in York.

The monarchs of Scotland and England, by their patronage of St Andrews, confirmed the status of the Cathedral and of the relics. In March 1304, three years before his death, Edward I (while attempting to crush the Scots with a ruthless military and political campaign), brought his second wife, Margaret (sister of Philip IV of France) to St Andrews. Perhaps as spiritual insurance, or to hedge their theological bets, they each offered a jewelled gold bracelet for the arm of St Andrew. The Queen's gift, on 19th March, was valued at seven merks. Four days later, the King presented a similar gift (valued at six merks).

Royalty continued the devotional tradition. In 1461 Queen Mary of Gueldres, influenced by Burgundian piety, visited the shrine, while the urbane and highly civilised James IV continually made offerings. Poet and herald, Sir David Lindsay, wrote that the King celebrated St Andrew's Day with great ceremony:

And ilk year for his Patron's saik,
Ane banquet royall wald he maik,
With wylde fowle, venisoun and wyne,
With tairt and falm and fruitage fyne;
Of bran and geill¹ there was na skant,   1: jelly
And ypooras² he wald not want.   2: from 'Hypocras' – mulled wine

James V and Marie de Lorraine were married in the Cathedral in June 1538 and it was in St Andrews that, a year later, the king's eldest son, James Stewart, was born.

There is some dispute over the relative importance of the Scottish shrines. To some extent, there was a fashion in saints and pilgrimage. The 'four heid pilgrimages' of Scotland (in order of importance during the reign of James IV) have been identified as St Ninian's *Candida Casa* (Whithorn), Tain (St Duthac), Whitekirk (Our Lady of the Hamer) and the Isle of May (the tomb of St Adrian). During the reign of James V, there are apparently only three 'heid pilgrimages' – Whithorn, Tain and St Andrews.

As for pilgrimage statistics, the only record of pilgrim numbers which has survived is a figure of 15,653 who came to Whitekirk in 1413. This figure is recorded in a document in the Vatican Library, a copy of which was brought back from Rome by Sir David Baird of Newbyth. One can only guess at the numbers who came to St Andrews.

In a letter to Pope Innocent X, James IV assures him that pilgrims from England, Ireland and the adjoining countries yearly flocked to Whithorn. Accordingly, a charter of James IV underlines the need to provide the bodily wants of pilgrims at Whithorn.

For the well-to-do, as Chaucer's 'Canterbury Tales' remind us, the journey to the shrine could be a flamboyant and entertaining affair. When in October 1504 James set out on pilgrimage to Tain, he did so accompanied by dogs and hawks and enjoyed sport on the way. He was entertained by four Italian minstrels; young girls performed dances and pipe-organs were carried in his retinue to be used at the divine service. Two years later, in very different circumstances – to pray for the Queen's recovery from childbirth – James made the journey from Edinburgh to Whithorn, apparently on foot.

There are at least two recorded cases where penitents were ordered to have recourse to the 'heid pilgrimages'. This they could do in person, or by proxy – by giving a stipend to a priest to celebrate a mass on their behalf. This was also one of the ways of providing a modest income for ordinary clerics.

John White of Edinburgh, in expiation of the crime of murder, agreed in May 1525 to pay the father of his victim one hundred marks, and to pay a priest to say requiem masses at Scala Coeli in Rome and at the four heid pilgrimages of Scotland. Five years later the feuding Kers and Scotts were to seek forgiveness by going to the four 'heid pilgrimages' of Scotland to arrange for masses to be celebrated for the soul of Andrew Ker of Cesford and those killed with him in the field at Melrose.

ST ANDREWS CATHEDRAL AND ST RULE'S TOWER

Chapter 9

St ANDREWS CATHEDRAL
AT THE
REFORMATION

THE Cathedral of St Andrews was the scene of many historic events. On 3 February 1414, for example, the church bells of the town rang to welcome the bulls of foundation of the privileges of the new University of St Andrews. They had been granted by the elderly pope, Benedict XIII, in his fortress-retreat of Peñiscola in Aragon, Spain.

After the bulls had been formally presented to Bishop Henry Wardlaw in the Augustinian priory, the diocesan clergy and the canons processed to the high altar of the Cathedral, reaching it just before the 10 am Mass was due to begin.

The day was spent in continuous rejoicing and at night, the streets of the town were lit up by bonfires.

Over a century later, in 1538, the French Princess Marie de Lorraine celebrated her marriage to James V at the cathedral with mass, singing and the playing of the organ. Afterwards the king and queen dined in the abbey accompanied by *shawms* (a tenor oboe), trumpets and other instruments. Sir David Lindsay of the Mount presented pageants which were interspersed with jousting and feasting.

It seems to have become customary to baptise princes of Scotland at St Andrews. In 1264, Alexander, son of King Alexander III, had been baptised by Gamelin, Bishop of St Andrews. Although the future James III was born in Stirling, it was not until two years later that he was baptised at St Andrews and his princely style proclaimed. Conversely, the king's eldest son was baptised at St Andrews in 1539 and named James Stewart, Duke of Rothesay and Prince of Scotland.

By the beginning of the sixteenth century, St Andrews had declined as a pilgrimage centre. The 1518 charter of St Leonard's College notes that *'the wonders for which the relics became famous brought so many pilgrims from diverse lands that a hospital* [hostel] *was built, but as the pilgrimages and miracles had in a measure ceased, so that the hospital was without pilgrims'*. The hospital was now to be converted into a college, along with St Leonard's church. The writer adds that the miracles at St Andrews had ceased because, in course of time, the Christian faith had established itself in Scotland – there was no longer any need for miracles to convert unbelievers or waverers.

The distinction between pilgrim and tourist was hard to see. Pilgrims were tourists, moving with little hindrance through international borders. This is well illustrated by the ease with which the professional manuscript-procurer, Marcus Wagner, an agent of the collector Flacius Illyricus, gained access to the Augustinian priory in 1553. He simply posed as a pilgrim calling at St Andrews on his way to Jerusalem and easily managed to steal some of the Augustinians' most precious volumes, including the St Andrews Music Book.

Heresy Trials and Assassination

But it was the heresy trials and executions staged at St Andrews Cathedral that would haunt the memory of the Reformers, as much as its role as a centre of administration or the wealth it contained.

On 23 July 1433, probably after a trial in the cathedral, Paul Kravar, a Wyclifite theologian and paramedic from Prague, was burned publicly at St Andrews.

Patrick Hamilton was tried for his Lutheran beliefs in the church and sentenced there almost a century later on 29 February 1527. His trial was presided over by Archbishop James Beaton and his nephew David Beaton.

Then Henry Forrest, after trial in the cathedral, was burned at the north church style in October 1533, so that all the people of Forfar could see the fire and be frightened from taking up the same doctrine.

Heresy trials were staged with studied formality. There would be tiers of seats for the dignitaries, erected against the chancel-screen. This intimidating phalanx rose above the platform where the prosecutor stood, dressed in a white surplice with a blood-red hood hanging down his back.

The accused was placed on another platform and the rest of the church was crammed with the devout and the curious, standing to watch the drama unfold.

The reformer George Wishart was tried in 1546 at the cathedral in front of Cardinal Beaton. The trial began with John Winram, sub-Prior of St Andrews, preaching from the prosecutor's platform on the parable of the Wheat and the Cockle – the final separation and burning of the alien and noxious growth. This was only a prelude to Wishart's death by fire on 1 March 1546. Wishart's execution persuaded many of the novices in the abbey, led by John Winram himself, to lean towards the Protestant faith.

Three months later, on 29 May, Cardinal David Beaton, Archbishop of St Andrews and Chancellor of Scotland, was murdered in his palace at St Andrews.

Ten years after, however, on 20 April 1558, John Winram was again amongst the bishops and abbots at the last heresy trial held in the cathedral, that of the last Scottish Protestant martyr, Walter Myln, parish priest of Lunan, who was then over eighty years of age.

Destruction of the Cathedral

Just over a year later, on Sunday 11 June 1559, John Knox entered St Andrews and preached in the parish church on the ejection of the buyers and sellers from the Temple. Knox preached for the next three days. On Wednesday 14 June 1559 the work of destruction began:

> *... they fell to purge the kirk and break down the altars and images and all kind of idolatrie ... and before the sun wes down there was never inch standing but bare walls. Bot the idols that were in the Abbay were brought to the north of the said Abbay ... and there they burned the whole idols.*

In a fitting irony, the images of the church were publicly burned on the very spot where Walter Myln had been cruelly executed by fire in April 1558.

This was a well-organised operation to destroy altars, images of saints, vestments, liturgical books and other equipment of the traditional liturgy – popularly referred to as the 'monuments of idolatrie'.

The furnishings of the Cathedral were broken and burnt. Nothing survives to show the quality of woodcarving or painting, manuscript illumination, stained glass or embroidery. Only a fine thirteenth century head of Christ and fragments of Bishop Wardlaw's tomb survived. Four centuries of liturgical worship came to an abrupt end.

All items of precious metal were removed before the raid and after it – bell-metal, brass lairs, lead, timber, slates and other building material would be removed by the prior, James Stewart, who was later to be assassinated at Linlithgow in 1570. On 6 January 1561, the silver-work, brass, ceremonial vestments and ornaments of the parish church were sold by public auction.

Geoffrey Barrow, former professor of Scottish History at Edinburgh University, comments (*The Scotsman*, 4 May 1991):

> *In its day St Andrews was as famous as St Thomas and Canterbury. I think probably you could say it was one of the most important half-dozen, or even three or four, in Northern Europe. I think it was wiped out at the Reformation. There is very little literature on this. There was a reluctance in the 18th and 19th centuries to take any of these things seriously because the ethos in Scotland was so strongly Protestant and Presbyterian.*

The revenues of the priory were siphoned off to the King until the death of James V, after which they seem to have gone to the young prior's mother, Margaret Douglas, at Lochleven.

In Scotland generally, the change from Roman Catholic to Reformed was not a dramatic one, but a very gradual process. The case of the population of St Andrews, which went to bed one evening as Roman Catholics and awoke the next morning to find themselves Protestants, was not typical.

The Scottish Reformation obliterated almost all of the evidence for the nature of popular devotion in Scotland. Today, such evidence is much harder to find than in England where church furnishings and monuments had been less thoroughly and systematically eradicated than in Scotland. However, it should be remembered that the Reformers, while stripping out the furnishings of churches, were careful to preserve the fabric of the buildings to be re-furbished as Reformed kirks. No substantial damage was done to the structure of St Andrew's Cathedral, for example, at the time of the Reformation.

In terms of human lives, the Scottish Reformation was much less violent than that in England, where some 300 Protestants were executed under Mary Tudor (1553-58) and around 156 Catholics under Queen Elizabeth (1558-1603). In Scotland 21 Protestants were executed before 1559 and three Catholic priests.

Yet no matter how 'velvet' it was, the systematic eradication of the Roman and papal theological and liturgical tradition took place all over Scotland. At Glasgow Cathedral images, paintings, glass and other 'relicks of popery' were destroyed. Only a few of the cathedral's treasures were spirited abroad by James Beaton, the last of the medieval archbishops. So complete was the expunging of the visible signs of the Roman rite that the only pre-Reformation image of St

Mungo still to be seen today is in Germany, at Cologne Cathedral.

On 29 June 1559 the army of the Lords of the Congregation entered Edinburgh. St Giles was pillaged and the altars destroyed. Jewels, silver vessels and vestments were sold by order of the magistrates and the proceeds used to pay for repairs to the fabric of the church. From that time the church was renamed the High Kirk of Edinburgh.

Some time after the Reformation the relic of St Giles – whose wooden statue had been previously burnt and sunk into the Nor' Loch – was taken out of its silver reliquary and deposited in the safe-keeping of the Dean of Guild. The diamond from the ring on its finger was sold and the arm-bone buried in St Giles kirkyard.

Destruction continued sporadically over the following years. At Holyroodhouse, six service-books of the chapel royal were burnt in 1569 by order of the Regent Moray, while four years later, the Regent Morton burned all the vestments and liturgical books of the town of Haddington.

John Winram and the Relics of St Andrew

Two of the key players in the disposal of the treasures of St Andrews Cathedral were Alexander Stewart, Prior of the Augustinian canons (one of the illegitimate sons of James V), and his sub-Prior, John Winram.

In 1544, as part of his 'Rough Wooing', Henry VIII ordered the destruction of the Bishops' Palace in St Andrews and the Cathedral. Stewart and Winram were instructed by Cardinal Beaton to remove the entire treasures of Cathedral and Palace to the safety of Portmoak priory by the shores of Loch Leven. Even though some of the Cathedral treasures were held in custodianship for the Scottish people, they were *de facto* the property of the Church authorities and it was the Cardinal's responsibility to ensure their safety.

Three of the chests contained relics and silk and gold cloths with various gear belonging to St Andrews which the canons placed for safety at Lochleven.

Apparently nothing was lost during this, the historical illustrator Jurek Pütter points out. This is interesting, because it was an almost predictable part of life in the Middle Ages that things 'got lost' or were appropriated. But everything taken to Portmoak was safely returned to St Andrews.

This was probably the first time in two centuries that the entire contents of the Cathedral, including the Great Morbrac, was moved to safety – which meant that Stewart, but Winram in particular, had the responsibility for overseeing it. They would draw up the inventory. These two people knew the entire contents of the Cathedral and the Bishop's Palace at first hand. They had practical experience of identifying, handling and packaging every artefact in the Cathedral treasure. That gave them a tremendous advantage, because probably they were the only people who knew the entire contents of the inventory which they themselves had drawn up. Thus, everything was safely brought back when the danger passed, for, instead of destroying the Bishops' Palace, Henry VIII's forces wrecked Dundee.

The exiled Roman Catholic historian, Ninian Winzet (1518-92), observed that John Winram was neither a good Catholic nor a good Protestant, but a damned good heathen. Winram was one of history's great snakes in the grass, comments Jurek Pütter. He was the type of great opportunist who, for example, had the Reformation not been successful, would have been one of the first to strut back onto the stage of history as the saviour of the relics of Andrew the Apostle.

Winram, a man who had devoted himself to chastity, charity and poverty, died a wealthy man. His gravestone still exists, much mutilated, at St Leonard's church in St Leonard's College.

The finger of suspicion points back to these two individuals who had very, very intimate knowledge and who had also managed the transportation of all of the relics – Alexander Stewart and John Winram. They were the two principal figures, when the Reformed religion consolidated itself, who were in material terms the absolute winners.

There is something to suggest, adds Jurek Pütter, that Winram, perhaps, removed the relics of Andrew the Apostle and so there is a strong possibility that a supreme manipulator like Winram would have had the relics built into a piece of furniture. This was a strategy often used in the later Middle Ages to safeguard great treasures. After Winram's death, there would be no need for the relics to be restored. In time, the relics in the furniture may have been dispersed or destroyed.

The Great Morbrac, the so-called 'twelve houses' (the house within a house within a house), was disposed of by Stewart and Winram. They effectively cut it up. Something of their wealth can be attributed to the cutting-up, melting-down, disposal of the gold, the silver, the precious and semi-precious stones.

Pütter argues:

It is a possibility that the relic in its hiding-place passed into the possession of his family and even survives today unrecognised in a kist [chest] or a dresser with a secret compartment. I do believe that the relics of St Andrew still exist. My hunch tells me that they still exist, not recognised or seen for what they really are. Stewart and Winram are one of the safest bets. They are highly unpleasant individuals and that makes them more interesting because their motives are much more discernible and transparent because of their duplicity.

In spite of the efforts of the Reformers to stamp out what they regarded as idolatrous superstitions, the urge to go on pilgrimage took some time to die. An Act of the Scottish Parliament of 1581 speaks of 'the perverse inclination to superstition through which the dregs of idolatry still remain in various parts of the realm by using pilgrimages to certain chapels, wells, crosses and other monuments of idolatry, as well as observing festival days of the saints, sometimes building bonfires or singing carols inside or around kirks'.

A Statute of 1593 makes it clear that travelling beggars were indistinguishable from pilgrims. Vagabonds and strong beggars pretending they were passing in pilgrimage to chapels and wells had become a public nuisance.

However, pilgrimage persisted stubbornly, even to such an unlikely place as Peebles, where the Holy Cross continued to be an object of veneration as it had been for James IV who had embellished the cross with precious metals.

An ordinance as late as 1599 was given to the minister of Innerleithen, William Sanderson, and some of the brethren, to await with certain gentlemen and baillies of Peebles to apprehend those who came in pilgrimage to the Cross Kirk. The band of vigilantes was duly successful in catching a number of local men and women who had come to pray in the old way.

Even two years later, it was necessary to take steps once more to turn pilgrims away. Persons who superstitiously went to the Cross Kirk at Beltane were to be apprehended by the magistrates and punished.

Chapter 10

IMAGES of
SAINT ANDREW

Patron of Scotland

THE historian George Buchanan records that St Andrew was looked upon as the patron saint of Scotland during the reign of Malcolm Canmore (1057-1093). It is likely that, from that period, St Andrew's Day would be celebrated as a national festival.

Events of national importance were deliberately held on 30 November – the coronation of John Balliol, for example, in 1292. After Balliol had been deposed, an English song told Scots to go to the Devil as St Andrew could no longer protect them.

From the early medieval period, St Andrew was the saint most likely to be called upon in time of war. In 1173 William the Lion swore by St Andrew that he would stay in England and fight for his heritage of Northumberland. There is little doubt that from that time, at least, 'St Andrew' was the battle-cry of the Scots.

The prayer of the Scottish patriot William Wallace (*circa* 1274-1305), according to the poet Blind Harry (*fl* 1470-92) in his *Acts and Deeds of Sir William Wallace*, was: 'St Andrew mot us speed.' And in 1303, before the battle of Roslin, Sir Simon Fraser addressed the Scottish leaders with the words: 'In God all your hope ye set; Saint Andrew, Saint Ninian and St Margaret.'

At the Battle of Bannockburn eleven years later, the Scottish soldiers wore the white cross of St Andrew on their tunics; and before the battle began, they knelt in prayer, invoking the protection of their patron saint.

This growing national consensus was given full public recognition when, four years later, Robert the Bruce, at the dedication of St Andrews Cathedral on 5 July 1318, placed a parchment at the High Altar expressing the nation's thanks for the victory at Bannockburn.

But it is the 'Declaration of Arbroath' (1320) which perhaps most urgently and completely asserts the integrity of the Scottish nation and its right to exist free from the threat of conquest by its belligerent southern neighbour.

Framed during a Scottish Parliament at Arbroath, at which the King and the Three Estates (clergy, nobility and burgesses) were present, the 'Declaration' gathered together what the Scots anticipated would be unassailable evidence and a pugnacious argument of Scotland's right to papal protection from the territorial ambitions of the English king.

It did so, cunningly, by first stressing the familial bonds between Scotland and the person of the Pope, John XXII ('Most holy father'; 'your obedient and devoted sons'). There followed a pungent reminder to Rome of the genealogy of the Scottish nation. By ancient tradition, the ancestors of the Scots were said to have been Scythians (Ukrainians) who had emigrated northwards through the Mediterranean Sea and then from the Atlantic seaboard of Spain.

And, while still in Scythia, it was the Scots (pointed out the Declaration) who were one of the first peoples to be evangelised by the first Apostle, Andrew. Based on the unverifiable accounts of the *Acts of Andrew*, this claim to be legitimate first-born followers of Christ asserted the fourteenth century Scots' right to be treated with positive discrimination by the Pope.

Next, the Scottish Parliament reinforced this claim by citing the ties of blood binding the successor of Peter to their forefathers on the shores of the Black Sea. On them, during his missionary labours in Scythia, Peter's brother Andrew had bestowed his personal patronage for all time.

Oppressed by the English king's looting and massacre in Scottish religious communities, and his cruel treatment of the Scottish people in general, the Scots bishops, nobility and burgesses, see their King Robert I as a new Maccabeus or a Joshua.

In investing their leader with the heroism of biblical figures, the Scots, after the triumph of Bannockburn, point to indisputable evidence of Divine support for their ventures, just as Eusebius did for Constantine, and Fordun and Bower for Óengus.

Maccabeus had taken command of the Jewish patriots in 166 BC, driven the enemy out, purified the Temple and restored the ancient worship of Jehovah. Joshua succeeded Moses as leader of the Israelites. After forty years of wandering through the desert, the people of Israel were led by Joshua into the promised land of Canaan.

In a Scottish context this implies that the centre of Scotland's military and religious power is now focused through the national church, the Cathedral of St Andrews.

The Scots then go on to suggest that aggression between Christian nations will damage the stability of the papacy and its credibility. Finally, they appeal to a cause dear to the Pope's heart – the Crusade. If Rome forces Edward to stop his incursions into Scotland, then both Scotland and England will be free to send men on the Crusade to liberate the Holy Places. The 'Declaration of Arbroath' was particularly effective in establishing Scotland's historical right to an independent identity and culture.

Even after the Reformation, St Andrew had a place of honour in the Scottish psyche. Andrew Melville (1545-1622), one of the leaders of the Scottish Reformation, nevertheless had considerable regard for Scotland's patron saint (and his own namesake), writing:

Saint Andrew, Christ's Apostle true
Does sign the Scotsmen's rites;
Saint George, Armenian heresiarch,
The Englishmen delights.
Let Scotsmen then hold fast the Faith
That is wholly apostolic,
Howbeit that England keeps the course
That is wholly apostatic.

The discrepancy between Saint George and Saint Andrew which so delighted Melville was diplomatically resolved on 15 March 1603 when King James VI and I, Queen Anne and Prince Henry solemnly processed from the Tower of London to Whitehall. There had, according to the entertainment scripted by the playwright Thomas Dekker (c. 1570-1632), been great apprehension that the country would be torn apart by civil war after the death of Elizabeth I.

But the 'feared wounds of a civil sword' were 'stopped from bursting forth by the sound of trumpets that proclaimed King James. All eyes,' writes Dekker, 'were presently turned north to behold this 45 years' wonder now brought forth by time'.

What the King and his new subjects in London saw was Dekker's extraordinary allegorical pageant. From opposite sides of the street appeared two knights on horseback and in full armour, draped with the heraldic arms of England and Scotland.

England's patron, Saint George, met an anachronistically warlike fisherman Andrew – now also in shining armour. They grasped hands before the crowds to 'testify their leagued combination and new sworn brotherhood' and so rode towards the King, both saints brought to life to signify the hoped-for political unity of a new nation.

Even that staunch supporter of the Treaty of Union, Sir Walter Scott, saw the unifying potential in St Andrew of Scotland. On 14 August 1822 he welcomed King George IV at Leith:

> *Sir Walter Scott was admitted on board the royal yacht and was graciously received by the King. The object was to present a St Andrew's cross to His Majesty, in the name of a party of distinguished ladies in Edinburgh, The Sisters of the Silver Cross.*
>
> *This cross was formed of pearls on blue velvet, within a belt of gold, on which was embroidered with pearls the following Gaelic motto, Riagh Albiam gu brath! – Hail to the King of Scotland! This elegant and costly emblem of Scotland was the work of Mrs Skene of Rubislaw, the sister of Sir William Forbes. It was graciously received by His Majesty and worn in his hat during his stay in Scotland.*

Russia

In Russia, the legend of their patron saint Andrew's visit continued to have great potency. The Russians and the Greeks maintained an uneasy relationship at the time of the Byzantine Empire. In the year AD 988 the Emperor Basil II had asked the Russian Prince Vladimir (*circa* 956-1015) for help. The latter dispatched an army of 6000 Russian mercenaries who arrived in Constantinople and managed to save the Emperor's throne. In the same year a mass baptism of Kievans took place in the waters of the river Dnieper.

From 1039, strong religious links between Russians and Byzantium were forged which were only broken when, in 1448, the Russian bishops severed their dependence on the Unionist primate of Constantinople and elected their own primate, making the Russian church a metropolitan diocese of the Byzantine Patriarchate.

Vladimir I's grandson, Vsevolod, founded the first Russian church dedicated to St Andrew, and had his own son, Vladimir Monomakh, take the baptismal name of Andrew. In addition, a grandson of Vsevolod (Andrey Dobryy, *died* 1142) and a great-grandson (Andrey Bogolyubskiy, *died* 1174) were the first Russian princes to be known by the name of Andrew.

As late as the sixteenth century, the Andrew legend persisted. In

1582, when Ivan the Terrible met the papal envoy Antonio Possevino in Moscow, he boasted that the Russians had received their Christian faith from St Andrew the Apostle on the shores of the Black Sea at the same time as Christianity first came to Rome. Even a century later, in 1698, Peter the Great created a Russian Order of knighthood, the Knights of the Blue Ribbon whose emblem was the St Andrew's Cross.

The Saltire Flag

The Saltire (Cross of St Andrew) is essentially a dynamic community icon, a multiplication sign, its diagonals expressing radical and restless action, in contrast to the timeless finality of the so-called 'Latin' cross with its 90 degree quarterings.

The word 'Saltire' comes from the Old French *saultoir*, itself derived from the Low Latin *saltatorium* which means 'stirrup', from the Latin *saltare* meaning 'to leap'. Like many English words, it has a long family tree, denoting much movement geographically, motivated by commerce, culture and war. It is a word which denotes action.

The Saltire is the Scottish National Flag and Arms, defined by Act of Parliament as Azure (sky blue), a Saltire Argent (silver). This is recorded in the Lyon Register (1672) as the 'Armes or Badge' proper and peculiar to the Kingdom of Scotland.

Although the flag and colours of Scotland are habitually rendered as white, the correct colour of the Saltire is silver. As silver paint tarnishes easily and silver thread is expensive, white is generally substituted. But it should be noted that the colour white does not exist in heraldry – it is the representation of silver metal. And, interestingly, the Royal Navy uses dark blue rather than Azure (sky blue) because it weathers better. The white Saltire on a red background is the English Neville family arms.

The Cross of St Andrew is the flag which any Scotsman is entitled to fly, or to wear as a badge, the emblem of his national identity or patriotism. It is also the proper flag to fly in Scottish churches.

One major problem in examining the use of the Saltire is the scarcity of Scottish heraldic records, many of which have not survived. Some were burnt at a fire in Perth in 1650, when the Lyon King, Sir James Balfour, was removing them for safety before the arrival of Oliver Cromwell. A second fire, about twenty years later, is believed to have destroyed the register at the Lyon Office. In addition, some 85 hogsheads of Scottish historical papers were lost at sea in 1661 while they were on their way back to Scotland from London where they had been taken by General George Monck.

The burgh crosses of Scotland, which date back to the time of William the Lion, were often decorated with the Saltire – this was the case in Inverness, Burntisland and Dunfermline, for example. In many cases the Saltire would be carried on a shield held by a unicorn.

One of the clearest statements of the importance of the Saltire to the Scots is to be found in the Acts of Parliament of Robert II of 1 July 1385. A Treaty between the kings of Scotland and France agreed that every Frenchman or Scot should wear a white St Andrew's Cross on his chest and on his back. If his jacket or his coat was white, he was required to wear the white cross on a piece of black cloth which could either be round or square. Black was specified rather than blue, to give the maximum contrast with the white jackets of the French. A similar order was issued in 1523.

The 'Great Michael', a ship built for James IV in 1511, was said to have been 73 metres in length, with 35 big guns and 300 small artillery. It was capable of carrying 300 sailors, 120 gunners and 1000 soldiers. This giant man-of-war, said at the time to be the largest warship in the world, was commanded by Sir Andrew Wood of Largo (*circa* 1460–1540). For its construction, most of the trees of Fife were said to have been cut down. The main standard of the vessel was the St Andrew's Cross on a blue ground.

Sir Andrew Barton, commander of the 'Lion' and a former pirate, destroyed many English ships. Finally, he lost both his ships in an engagement with Sir Edward Howard whom Henry VIII had sent against him. As he lay dying in 1511, Barton encouraged his men with the words:

> *'Fight on, my men,' Sir Andrew says,*
> *'And never flinch before the foe,*
> *And stand fast by St Andrew's Cross,*
> *Until you hear my whistle blow.'*

Although the cross of St Andrew was silver on a blue background, it might be displayed over any colour or mixture of colours – in the 1540s ships' ensigns were flown with white crosses over the Royal colours of red and yellow.

But, later, James VI (King of England 1603–1625), issued a proclamation to his naval forces that 'our subjects of North Britain shall wear in their foretops the white cross only as they were accustomed'.

The *Accounts of the Lord High Treasurer* for August 1513 records the fever of activity with which the Scots prepared for the Battle of Flodden. Not only were cloth and fringes ordered, but extra payments were made to expedite the contract (*eg* 'Item for making of them in haste 4/-').

Several Scottish standards survive. The Douglas Standard was said to have been carried at the Battle of Otterburn (1388) by Archibald Douglas, second Earl of Douglas. It is of green silk with a number of devices painted onto the cloth, one being a white St Andrew's Cross, now oxidised to black.

The Marchmont Standard seems to have been the flag of the Warden of the Marches in the sixteenth century. It bears a St Andrew's Cross, as does the 'Blue Blanket' of Edinburgh, said to have been given to the Incorporated Trades of the city by James III and his queen, Margaret. The flag of the Incorporated Trades of Stirling is light blue and shows the white Saltire.

During the Battle of Carberry Hill, the forces of the Queen displayed the Saltire, while at the siege of Edinburgh Castle in 1572-73, both the defender, Kirkcaldy of Grange and the Regent Morton flew the Saltire.

After the Reformation, there was an understandable decline in interest in saints and their days. However, John Knox's Liturgy – the *Book of Common Order,* contains the names of many saints.

In 1621, a charter granted under the Great Seal of Scotland was given to Sir William Alexander for the colonisation of Nova Scotia. The ensigns armorial of this colony consisted of a silver shield with a blue St Andrew's Cross. Eight years later, the King authorised the Baronets of Nova Scotia to wear a personal decoration with the same blue Saltire.

Whether they were Roman Catholics serving the King of France or Protestants fighting for Gustavus Adolphus (with his four Scottish generals and 22 Scottish colonels), Scots always carried the Saltire. The Douglas regiment, which entered the service of Louis XIII of France in 1634 (later the 1st Royal Scots), also bore the Scottish national flag.

Even after the Reformation, the religious significance of the Saltire was well understood and the flag of the Apostle came to symbolise the distinct Scottish identity. When in 1639 the Scots (incensed by the King's attempts to introduce an English style of worship into Scotland) prepared to fight King Charles I, it is recorded that every captain in the Scottish army had 'a colour with the Scottish arms and an inscription in golden letters: FOR CHRIST'S CROWN AND COVENANT'.

After the Scots were defeated at Preston (1648) and Dunbar (1650), many of their flags were captured by the English. Of the 223 flags which fell into the hands of the English and were recorded in drawings now in the British Museum, no less than 150 contained the Saltire.

At state funerals the Saltire was given a place of honour. At the funeral of Mary Queen of Scots, James VI and even Oliver Cromwell, the Saltire was prominently displayed. In Cromwell's case, it is described as 'Azure, a Saltire Argent'.

At sea the Saltire continued to be a means of provocation to the English. In 1639, for example, a Scottish ship was arrested in the Thames for hanging out the 'Scotch flag of St Andrew'.

The Order of the Thistle, revived during the reign of James VII, had been previously known as the Order of St Andrew. On the badge of the Order there appears the figure of the Saint in a green gown and purple surcoat, carrying a white enamelled cross. The Star of the Order is a silver Saltire with rays radiating from the arms, echoing the blinding vision of the morning sun seen by Óengus and his army at Athelstaneford.

Today, the ribbon of the Order is green, from the colour of the Thistle. The original colours were those of the national flag – blue and white. The Jewel, worn by the Dean of the Order, is oval in shape and carries a plain Saltire. It belonged to James VII (1633-1701). In the centre of the Jewel is an oval *chalcedony* (two-coloured precious stone) cut with a cameo of St Andrew with his cross. The figure of the Saint is white, while the background is a bluish grey.

But the revival of the Order in 1688 did not meet with universal approval. Describing the events, Gilbert Burnett (1643-1715), Bishop of Salisbury, wrote: 'They broke into all popish chapels, and into the church of Holy Rood House, which had been adorned at a great charge to be a royal chapel, particularly for the Order of St Andrew and the Thistle.'

In the field of commerce, Scots also used the image of St Andrew. In one of the most ill-fated of their ventures, five ships of the Company of Scotland trading to Africa and the Indies (The Darien Scheme) sailed from Leith on 17 July 1698. One of the armed ships was the 'St Andrew'. At their arrival on the Isthmus of Panama, the Scots constructed Fort St Andrew as a fortress for their colony of New Caledonia.

More successful were the Scottish financial institutions at home.

The Saltire is prominent in the arms of the Bank of Scotland, the Royal Bank of Scotland, the Edinburgh Merchant Company (1693), and the Company of Linen Manufacturers of Scotland (1694). It is prominent in the crest of the Royal College of Surgeons, Edinburgh, the Society of Antiquaries of Scotland, and Writers to Her Majesty's Signet.

Many historic regiments displayed the Saltire – the Royal Scots, the King's Own Scottish Borderers, the Black Watch, the Highland Light Infantry, the Gordon Highlanders, and the Cameron Highlanders. The Queen's Bodyguard for Scotland, the Royal Company of Archers, also carry the figure of St Andrew on his cross.

After the Union of the Parliaments in 1707, the St Andrew's Cross was to some extent replaced by the Union Flag. However, during the 1715 Jacobite Rising, the Saltire came into its own again.

Lady Kenmure had embroidered her husband's blue flag with a golden Saltire when he led his men from Galloway to fight for the Old Pretender. The Saltire was also flown by an Edinburgh volunteer unit on the Government side, using a flag said to have been carried at the Battle of Bothwell Brig (1679).

It is interesting that even for Jacobites abroad, Andrew maintained his position as spiritual lynchpin of the Scottish nation. On 30 November 1717, for example, although exiled in Italy, the Old Pretender, Prince James Francis Edward Stewart – 'James III' – made a conscious effort to attend the service of Benediction at the church of St Andrew the Apostle in Urbino to observe the requirements of the holy-day:

As the morning of that day was the Festival of the Apostle and His Majesty had made his devotions, because the said Saint is the Protector of Scotland, that evening he did not hold a reception.

At the Battle of Culloden, the final act of the 1745 Rising, the Appin Clan regiment's colours escaped the conflict. It is made from light blue silk with a yellow Saltire. In Edinburgh, the flag used from 1676-1789 by the first company of the City Trained Bands was a white Saltire on a blue background.

In the United States, the flag of the American Colonies, with its thirteen stripes and the old Union Flag in the corner, had the English part of the Union Flag removed in 1777, leaving the Scottish colours. Even one of the flags used by the Confederate side in the American Civil War had its stars arranged in the form of the St Andrew Cross (the Southern Cross – Gules, on a Saltire azure).

Seals

Of the Scottish heraldic records which survive, the wax seals used to authenticate official documents reveal a considerable amount about the symbolism and self-image of Scotland.

Since it is a general principle of heraldry that a simpler form precedes a more complex one, it is probably safe to assume that the stylised and non-representational Saltire was used as a symbol before the crucified figure of St Andrew was adopted.

The Saltire would have been in use, therefore, before the first known representation in Scotland of St Andrew crucified: on the Seal of the Guardians of Scotland (1286-92), where it is accompanied by the motto: 'Andrew, be the leader of your compatriots, the Scots', probably referring to the fact that the Saltire was routinely carried by the Scots into battle.

In due course, however, the naturalistic figure of the crucified Saint became the norm. In the 13th century, the seal of Bishop Gamelin, chaplain to Alexander III and Chancellor of Scotland (1254), shows St Andrew being tied to his cross. Bishop William Fraser's seal (Chancellor 1274-1280), has the Apostle tied by his arms to a Saltire cross. That of James Bane (Bishop of St Andrews, 1328-1332) elaborates by having St Andrew being tied to his cross by four men, two of them climbing up on ladders to lash his arms to the wood.

Although the thistle as a badge dates from the reign of James III (1488-1513), the silver cross of the Saltire is the authentic badge of Scotland. It appears on the seals of James I and James II and on that of Queen Mary of Gueldres, founder of Trinity College, Edinburgh. In the fifteenth century, a Saltire appears on the seal of the vicar-general of St Andrews.

Post-Reformation seals of the dioceses of St Andrews, Dunblane, Caithness, and Edinburgh, all carry the Saltire. It is worth noting that two English cathedral-sees, dedicated to St Andrew, carry the Saltire in their arms – the see of Rochester and that of Wells. The badge of the Conservator of Scottish Privileges in the Netherlands (an office dating from before 1444) contains a small shield with the figure of St Andrew. In the middle of the fourteenth century, the same figure of St Andrew was being used by the Scottish students' union at the University of Orleans.

Under Cromwell's rule, an order was made on 22 April 1654 that 'the Arms of Scotland, *viz* a cross commonly called St Andrew's

Cross', should be carried by all public seals, seals of office, and seals of bodies civil or corporate in Scotland.

Coins

Early Scottish coins usually have the head of the sovereign on one side and a cross (sometimes a Saltire) on the other. David II (1329-71) issued the first Scottish gold coin – the *noble* – with a St Andrew's Cross on the reverse. The Scottish *noble* is a direct copy of a similar English coin which bears the Cross of St George. This is evidence that at this period the Saltire was regarded as Scotland's national emblem.

A series of coins issued by succeeding Scottish kings were known as 'St Andrews' from the Saltire and the saint on the reverse. Gold crowns of James V (1513-42) carry on the obverse a royal shield with a Saltire on each side, perhaps symbolising the support of the king by the people; while the bawbee of this period displays a Saltire with a royal crown at the junction of the arms.

Gold crowns of Mary Queen of Scots (1542-87) are closely modelled on those of her father, James V. The six pound piece of James VI (1567-1625), however, carries a sword and sceptre in the form of a St Andrew's Cross. The Saltire *plack* (coin) also has two crossed sceptres. The Grenadier Guards still carry the sword and sceptre crossed in this way as a regimental badge. It is described as a device used by the House of Stuart.

It is interesting, in this context, to note the papal arms on the scabbard of the Scottish Sword of State. A gift from Pope Julius II to James IV, it was presented to the king at Holyrood on Easter Sunday 1507. Between the three-tiered crown and the papal shield are the symbolic keys of papal authority, crossed Saltire-fashion and wrapped with criss-cross bindings, recalling the Roman imperial *fasces*, representing authority and retribution.

From the Union of the Crowns in 1603, coins issued by the Scottish mint rarely carried national emblems, perhaps out of sensitivity to the unifying aspirations of the monarch in London.

In 1626, the Scottish Privy Council noted that the seals for use in Scotland carried the Royal Arms quartered in the English manner and ordered them to be broken and new ones made. Two centuries later, the Royal Arms (which carried the English three leopards in the place of honour), displayed on Edinburgh's General Post Office were removed at the instigation of Lyon Depute and the usher of the white rod as 'derogatory to the independence of Scotland'.

Some of the copper coins of Charles I and Charles II had the four shields arranged to make the shape of a Saltire. Among the coins issued by James VII was a ten-shilling piece with a St Andrew's Cross on the reverse. Broadly speaking, the Royal Arms have continued to be used in the coinage of the realm by the House of Stuart, the House of Hanover, and the House of Windsor.

Sculpture, Painting and Stained-glass

In painting, sculpture and stained-glass, St Andrew was popularly seen as an old bald man with one or two books in his hand – probably the *Acts of Andrew*. Traditionally he is presented as a fisherman shown with fish, a fishing-net or a rope, or sometimes with a boat.

St Andrew was imagined to have been the founder of the Byzantine patriarchate in opposition to the Roman papacy founded by St Peter. But only the Greek and Syriac Churches recognised this claim.

The apocryphal *Acts of Andrew* were used by the heretical Gnostics and Manicheans to oppose the canonic teaching of the New Testament, and it was from the elaborate adventures in the *Acts of Andrew* that the image of Andrew's crucifixion was taken, not from the Gospels.

Andrew makes a relatively late appearance in Christian art. In the Greek East only his crucifixion is shown; in the Latin West an edited, less exaggerated, version of the *Acts of Andrew* was used as source-material. In the Afro-Asian Churches, however, a wealth of miracle stories exist about Andrew. There, from earliest times, the Apostle was unashamedly used as a vehicle of propaganda.

A fifth century Egyptian catacomb preserves the image of Andrew and Philip feeding the five thousand. From the sixth century onward, Andrew's dishevelled white hair and beard distinguish his portraits. He is often shown directing the feeding of the multitude and – as in the mosaics from the church of San Apollinare Nuovo in Ravenna – in the company of Peter at the moment of their calling.

A head of Andrew dating from the eighth century can be found in Santa Maria Antiqua in Rome. By the ninth century, Andrew appears in a number of Byzantine miniatures in manuscripts – such as the *Codex of Homilies* of Gregory of Nazianus, or a Greek *menologion* (calendar of saints) today in the Vatican Library. On both these miniatures, Andrew is nailed to his cross. It is in ninth century Byzantine manuscripts that the first series of crucifixions of Andrew show him on the Latin cross, nailed but not tied (contrary to the description in the *Acts of Andrew*), with others present to witness his final hour.

The famous X-shaped cross makes its appearance first on a *troparium* (hymn book) from Autun, which is probably of tenth century manufacture. During that and the succeeding century, in the margins of *psalters* (prayer-books of the psalms), Andrew is depicted preaching and baptizing. He also appears among other saints on carved ivories of this period.

In a *sacramentary* (service book) at Ivrea, made about the year 1000, Andrew is shown in the centre of the picture, on his cross, while to his left stands a military executioner tying him to it.

On the eleventh century bronze doors of the basilica of San Paolo fuori le Mure in Rome, Andrew is depicted nailed to a Y-shaped cross. From the twelfth century dates a statue of Andrew at Amalfi, Italy, while in thirteenth century glass paintings in Troyes and Auxerre in France, Andrew is shown chasing away demons in the form of dogs.

The fifteenth century is distinguished by Hugo van der Goes (*died* 1482) who created the magnificent Trinity Altarpiece showing King James III of Scotland being protected by St Andrew.

Papal recognition of the importance of St Andrew to the Scots can be seen today in the sceptre which forms part of the Honours of Scotland. Presented to James IV by Pope Alexander in 1494, its complex design includes a statuette of St Andrew with his cross.

Many of the greatest Renaissance painters chose to include St Andrew in their work – Fra Angelico (*circa* 1387-1455), Andrea Mantegna (*circa* 1431-1506), Tintoretto (1518-94) and El Greco (1541-1614) all used St Andrew in their compositions. The best-known image of St Andrew is perhaps that of Leonardo da Vinci's (1452-1519) 'Last Supper' (1497), painted on the wall of Santa Maria delle Grazie, Milan, where Andrew can be seen sitting third from the left end of the table.

One of Leonardo's most potent anatomical studies is the pen and ink drawing of the 'Vitruvian Man', a drawing (made around 1485-90) of a nude male figure standing and stretching in a T-formation inside a square and then repeating the movement with his arms raised and his legs spread out inside a circle in what is virtually the familiar X-cross of St Andrew. The drawing was made to illustrate a passage in *De Architectura*, the only surviving Roman treatise on architecture, written by Marcus Vitruvius Pollio, an architect and military engineer in the service of the Emperor Augustus, but perhaps we can also see the Andrew of legend in the design. By Leonardo's time, the 'Cosmological Man' was a traditional figure even of astrological importance.

For Leonardo, Man was the model of the world and the human body was constructed on the framework of a square and a circle. All architecture was for Leonardo, as for the architects of Classical Greece, based on the harmonious proportions of the human body, the Golden Section upon which the plans of their finest temples were based.

Sixteenth century Germany also found St Andrew a significant figure, represented in such work as the anonymous painting (now in the National Galleries of Scotland) of the Saint with the donor's wife and children. A fine wood carving by Tilman Riemenschneider (*circa* 1460-1531) is on display in the Samuel H Kress Collection at the Atlanta Art Association Galleries, Atlanta, Georgia.

One of the best-known seventeenth century paintings of the Apostle is 'The Martyrdom of St Andrew' by Bartholomé Murillo (1617-82), now in Madrid. But for sheer size, it is the colossal statue of St Andrew in St Peter's, Rome which catches the eye. It was carved around 1629 by the Flemish sculptor François Duquesnoy, after he and Gian Bernini had completed the *baldachino* (canopy) which stands in front of one of the four great piers supporting the dome of St Peter's. A near copy now languishes in the municipal garden-centre at St Andrews, Fife – an unwanted gift which has become the source of some civic embarrassment.

Paradoxically, considering that St Andrew was once used by the Patriarchs of Constantinople as a means of rivalling the status of Rome, it is in Rome that many of the major monuments associated with the Apostle are to be found.

Lovers of classical music will recall that it was in 1678, at Sant' Andrea delle Fratte on the Via Capo le Case, the composer Alessandro Scarlatti (1659-1725) was married. In medieval times, Sant' Andrea delle Fratte had been a resting-place for Scottish pilgrims. The staff wore purple, hence the purple *soutanes* (robes) of Scots students at the Pontifical Scots College today. Sant' Andrea delle Fratte has a long association with pilgrims from Scotland and is now the Roman church of the Scottish Cardinal Thomas Winning.

In the church are large and dramatic mural paintings of the death of St Andrew (Lazzaro Baldi) and the Crucifixion of St Andrew (G B Leonardi). In similar vein at Sant' Andrea al Quirinale (built by Gian Bernini in 1678) can be seen a high altarpiece of the Crucifixion of St Andrew by Bogognone.

Sant' Andrea al Ponte Milvio (*Ponte Molle*) was erected by Pius II in 1462 on the spot where he met Cardinal Bessarion who brought the head of St Andrew received from Thomas Palaeologus.

The church was remodelled in the fifteenth century by Pope Nicholas V (who added the watch-towers) and was restored in 1805 by Pius VII, who commissioned Valdier to erect the triumphal arch at the entrance. Blown up by Garibaldi to arrest the advance of the French, it was again restored in 1850 by Pius IX.

The most significant event in the story of the cult of St Andrew occurred in 1461 with the arrival of the head of St Andrew in Rome. The Greek silver-gilt reliquary containing St Andrew's head had been taken from the Church of St Andrew, Patras in 1460 by the Despot of Morea, Thomas Palaeologus, and brought to Rome the following year.

The Byzantine reliquary is a primitive, elongated egg-shaped head with bearded features in very low relief, surmounted by a gem studded metal garland. The reliquary is in two halves which are hinged at the back of the skull. After it was handed back to the Orthodox Church by Pope Pius VI in 1962, it was replaced by a less representational reliquary, shaped like a church and more in keeping with current Orthodox practice.

A pen and ink drawing attributed to Ventura Salimbeni depicts the scene when Pius II received St Andrew's head at the Ponte Molle. Today the drawing is held in Florence at the Museo Horne. In addition, three marble reliefs by Paolo Romano showing two angels supporting St Andrew's head are in the Grotte Vaticane, Rome.

From Paolo Romano's sculptures and his statue of St Andrew standing outside Sant' Andrea al Ponte Milvio, it is clear that the head was transferred from the Greek silver gilt reliquary to Simone da Firenze's silver gilt reliquary for the public reception of the head by Pius II in Rome.

Da Firenze's reliquary head is highly realistic but heavily ornamented. It stands on substantial shoulders set above a broad decorated base. Behind the head is fixed a sunburst set inside a halo. There is a flamboyant carrying-handle shaped like a swordfish on each shoulder. The reliquary is to be seen today in Pienza, at the Museo del Duomo.

Sant' Andrea della Valle, Rome, built in 1591 from a design by Francisco Grimaldi and Giacomo della Porta, is especially associated with the Piccolomini family.

The Theatine Order's church and convent of Sant' Andrea della Valle had been founded on the site of the Piccolomini palace. The Palazzo di Siena, as it was popularly called, had been built by Cardinal

Piccolomini between 1460 and 1472. It had since been the head-quarters of the Piccolomini family in Rome.

In 1582 it passed into the hands of Costanza, the widowed Duchess of Amalfi, descended through her father from Pius II's nephew Andrea. Costanza was the last of her line. The Duchy of Amalfi had already passed into other hands and in 1610 she herself died at a convent in Naples.

Domenichino (1581-1641) filled the apse of Sant' Andrea delle Valle with key scenes from the life of St Andrew – John the Baptist pointing out Jesus to Andrew; Jesus calling Andrew; the executioners torturing Andrew; Andrew worshipping the Cross; Andrew being carried to Heaven by the angels.

In 1610 the Chapel of St Andrew at St Peter's Basilica was demol-ished by Paul V to make room for new construction in St Peter's.

The bodies of the two Piccolomini Popes were moved there from St Peter's in 1623. The marble reliefs from the tomb of Aeneas Sylvius Piccolomini (Pius II), are attributed to Paolo Romano.

Sant' Andrea della Via Flaminia (a small round church constructed by Jacopo Vignola 1550-55) was erected by Pope Julius III to commem-orate his deliverance from the Emperor Charles V's soldiers during the Sack of Rome in 1527.

San Spirito in Sassia was founded in AD 726 for Saxon pilgrims by Ine, King of Wessex, who died in Rome in the same year. Part of the arm of St Andrew had been given by Pius II to San Spirito in Sassia. In 1540 the church was rebuilt by Sangallo the Younger.

San Gregorio Magno on the Coelian Hill was originally built by Gregory the Great on the site of his father's house and dedicated to St Andrew. It was in the church in AD 596 that St Augustine bade farewell to St Gregory before setting out to England.

A new church dedicated to St Gregory was rebuilt on the site in the seventeenth and eighteenth centuries. In the centre of the church is the Chapel of Sant' Andrea with paintings of the Flagellation of St Andrew by Domenichino and St Andrew on the road to his Cross by Guido Reni.

In the chapel of Santa Barbara is a fresco by Antonio Viviani (1602) depicting the 'Non Angli sed angeli' incident which led to the Augus-tinian mission to England.

St Andrew's Church of Scotland, Rome, on the Via XX Settembre, one of ten charges within the Presbytery of Europe, was founded in 1862 by Scots and Americans. The Revd David Huie, Minister of St Andrew's, explained:

There is no St Andrew's Society or Caledonian Society in Rome.

We have a St Andrew's service on the Sunday nearest to St Andrew's Day to which the British ambassador and representatives of the Scots College are invited. We usually follow this with a congregational lunch. On one occasion a couple of years ago, our efforts to advertise this service with a notice: 'Are there any Scots out there in Rome?' appeared as 'Are there any Scouts out there in Rome?' The original question remained unanswered.

The Pontifical Scots College, Rome (founded by Pope Clement VIII in 1600) normally marks St Andrew's Day with a Mass in the present College chapel, followed by a lunch. In 1995 the Mass was held in Sant' Andrea delle Fratte. The congregation was addressed by the Very Revd Professor Robert Davidson and the new Cardinal Thomas Winning was guest of honour at the Scots College lunch which followed.

Contemporary Art

It is possible to identify some innovative uses of the Saltire in twentieth century art: Josef Hartwig's Bauhaus chess set, for example. Made from lacquered wood, it was mass-produced from 1923. The shape of each piece is determined by its move. The bishop is represented by a deep Saltire cut out of the square black chesspiece. The Saltire indicates the way in which the bishop moves diagonally with reference to the edge of the board. The chess set was very popular and every set, made from pearwood in natural and black finishes, was carved by hand.

Similarly in architecture: in *The Radiant City* (1933), the revolutionary French architect Le Corbusier observes: 'Human creation is a work of art. On the one hand, nature: a cone opening away from us towards infinity. Its point transfixes us; its contents are always flowing into us .... On the other hand, another cone, also opening away towards infinity: human creation. Between the two cones, where their points meet, stands man. Man the perceiver and man the revealer: the focal point.'

This is the significance of the Saltire.

'THE BLUE BLANKET' (DETAIL)

Chapter 11

THE SCOTTISH DIASPORA

OUTSIDE Scotland there are some 35 million people of Scottish descent. To meet the needs of Scottish ex-patriots as well as Scots in the British Isles, the World Federation of Scottish Societies and individuals was formed in Edinburgh on 24 March 1959. The aims of the Federation were:

- to maintain and preserve the rich heritage of Scotland's traditions and culture;
- to offer to Scots, and those of Scots descent from overseas, a centre of welcome and friendship from the Scots at home;
- to foster a closer bond of fellowship between all Scots and people of Scots descent around the world.

In Scotland itself, the St Andrew Society, a non-political body, was founded in 1907. Based in Edinburgh, the Society now incorporates the World Federation of Scottish Societies. Its aims are:

- to uphold the rights and privileges of Scotland and of the Scottish people as laid down under the Treaty and Acts of 1707 and other pertinent legislation;
- to secure that the proper nomenclature shall be used in all references to the Commonwealth of Nations, to the Monarchy, Navy, Army, Air Force, or any other part of the public services, and that, in all flags and heraldic symbols, Scotland shall have and retain the position to which she is entitled;
- to encourage the celebration of St Andrew's Day (30 November) as Scotland's National Day;
- to encourage the study of Scottish languages, history, literature, music and to support any movement which is favourable to the continuance of Scottish customs, sports, dancing, dress, arts and crafts and the like;

- to support by all means at its disposal, Scottish institutions;
- to receive into affiliation Scottish societies at home and abroad in order to further the Society's objects, and, in particular, to maintain connection with people of Scottish descent who may be living furth of Scotland;
- to maintain, in the capital of Scotland, premises as headquarters or club;
- to take such steps as the Council may consider necessary to preserve the national character of the Scottish people.

Among the activities undertaken by the Society has been an ongoing campaign to encourage the celebration of St Andrew's Day. A Flag Committee has carried out surveys to ascertain the reaction of local councils and firms to flying the Saltire on 30 November. The Scottish Flag Trust has been responsible for spotlighting the Saltire, for refurbishing the memorial plaque in Athelstaneford kirkyard and establishing a new visitor centre there.

The functions of the now-defunct World Federation have now fallen on the St Andrew Society. Affiliation to the St Andrew Society is regarded by many St Andrew and Caledonian societies as a mark of recognition. On St Andrew's Day the Society sends out greetings and a sprig of heather to all affiliates and receives telegrams and cards of greetings in return. The annual newsletter is sent out to all members and affiliates.

On the principle that the groundwork has to be laid early, the Society's *Schools' St Andrew's Day* competition presents a number of awards to schools for originality and variety in interpreting the meaning of St Andrew and his Day. These consist of plaques and Saltire flags.

In 1994, the main winner of the competition was Denny Primary School. There all 250 pupils took part in a parade headed by flag-bearers, and all the boys from the school called Andrew attended a service at Denny Parish Church. Then the pupils returned to school for an open day.

During the afternoon the pupils performed a new dance called 'St Andrew of Denny', which involved the pupils, dressed in their blue sweatshirts, forming four blue triangles of the Saltire and others (dressed in white) dancing along the diagonals. Pupils also designed a new logo for the school and the winning design incorporated a Saltire.

This was followed by a narration of the 'fishers of men' Gospel story told in the Scots tongue. Headteacher Miss Elizabeth Snaddon commented:

> *I think it is important that the children know there is a patron saint and are aware that it is not just any other day .... What we do gives the children enjoyment, but the activities also cover every aspect of the curriculum. We want to make sure it is a special day for them.*

The year before (1993) it was Parkside Primary School, Jedburgh which won. Headteacher Ken Fotheringham explained:

> *Like many schools, we have a concert on St Andrew's Day and sing Scots songs with performances of a variety of kinds – the story of St Andrew in word and picture; Scottish games, Scottish dances and a play about Robert Louis Stevenson with poems.*
>
> *The programme naturally varies from year to year and we have outside adult performers and a piper. Children are given Saltire stickers and short-bread.*
>
> *In 1993, we had a school competition with a 'Make a St Andrew's Day Card' challenge. Each class won a prize for their best entry. A Primary Six class made up a questionnaire and asked people on 30 November in Jedburgh High Street if they knew it was St Andrew's Day? Would they send a St Andrew's Day card if such were available? The response was mixed. Not everyone realised it was St Andrew's Day and not everyone promised to send cards! But it was a worthwhile exercise.*
>
> *Each year the St Andrew Society sends out information about St Andrew and the Athelstaneford vision to schools and this has raised the profile of the day.*

Another important organisation is the Saltire Society. Founded in 1936, the idea for the Saltire Society arose during a conversation between George Malcolm Thomson and Professor Andrew Dewar Gibb.

The object of the Society is as follows:

- to advance the education of the public by fostering and enriching the cultural heritage of Scotland in all its aspects, including the Scots and Gaelic languages;
- by looking to the future as well as the past and encouraging creativity in Scotland as a living element of European civilisation;
- by being concerned with all aspects of Scottish life at home and

abroad and by giving expression to the views of the Society as necessary within the constraints that it has no party political or sectarian affiliation;
- by co-operating with other institutions on matters, issues or undertakings which conform with the object of the Society.

As well as publishing books with its own imprint, the Saltire Society adjudicates and administers a number of awards in the fields of history, architecture, civil engineering and planning, fine art, science, literature, education and Scots song.

The Society strives to encourage anything that will improve the quality of life in Scotland and restore the country to its proper place as a creative force in European civilisation. The Society also seeks to revive the memory of famous Scots and to make the nation conscious of its heritage.

★   ★   ★

Perhaps the greatest concentration of St Andrew Societies is to be found in the United States. In Charleston, South Carolina on 30 November 1729, the world's first **Society of Saint Andrew** was formed. Founded by immigrant Scots, many from Aberdeen and Fife, the Society was dedicated to the relief of suffering and distress among inhabitants of the infant colony.

Today, St Andrew's Feast Day is the prime event of the **St Andrew's Society of North Carolina**, although it is never celebrated on 30 November. That date is too close to the national holiday of Thanksgiving, a time when families come together usually for a Thursday to Sunday long weekend. As a practical matter, the Society celebrates the Saint's Day on the Saturday following the Thanksgiving weekend. This is usually on a date in early December. For many, this constitutes the start of the Christmas season.

There is another small problem. Most members believe that 30 November is the birthday of the Saint. They have to be reminded constantly that it is a Feast Day, established by the early Church, and that the birth date of the Saint is unknown.

The Society holds the annual St Andrew's Day Banquet which is open to all members and their guests. The Society has male members only. A prominent speaker with a strong Scottish background is the main feature with a small pipe band as part of the entertainment. The programme could also have singers and dancers in place of a featured speaker. Attendance at these banquets runs to 160 or more. The Dinners are held in a resort area central to the state of North Carolina. The program includes the 'Salute to the Haggis', 'Toasts to the Saint, the Queen and the President', and a 'Report from Brother Scots'.

Each year on or around 30 November, members of **Fredericton Society of Saint Andrew** (founded 1825) have a Saint Andrew's dinner with friends and family. The program consists of a recital by the Fredericton Society of St Andrew Pipe Band. Following the conclusion of the pipes and drums entertainment, dinner is served at an appropriate time and the Haggis is piped in.

A pre-selected person recites the 'Address to the Haggis', and as the Society has an excellent haggis-maker, guests and members are extremely complimentary. At a suitable moment the President introduces the Speaker.

Unfortunately in recent years there has been no reference to St Andrew. While there have been no vociferous complaints about this sad omission, a few members have expressed their dismay about this neglect of Scotland's Patron Saint. Members hope that the Society executive will 'get the message' and alert future speakers to inject a solid reference to St Andrew.

On the Sunday following the St Andrew's dinner, members appear at St Andrew's Presbyterian Church and participate in Divine service given by the Society chaplain.

The Society has both male and female members. Total membership is about 200.

An early example of the Society's charity was John Campbell, whose case was considered in November 1826. Campbell was in distress for clothing. The Society provided him with a pair of trousers, a shirt, a yard of broad cloth, a comforter, shoes, socks, and a Scotch bonnet.

A widow, a native of Scotland, had three children, including two orphans of her sister. One of her children was dying from consumption. She lived in very poor circumstances and was helped by the Society in the 1860s by being given eight dollars.

The first dinner of the Society in 1826 seems to have been a gargantuan affair with 22 toasts! Unfortunately the bill of fare has not survived. It began with a dirge in pious memory of St Andrew, followed by 'God Save the King'. The second dinner, a year later, is faithfully recorded in great detail. Among the meats of the first course were boiled fowls, roast fowls, tongue, loin of veal, leg of mutton, haggis, boiled ham. The vegetables included mashed potatoes, turnips, boiled onions, beets and carrots.

The second course offered mince pies, tarts, whips, apple pies, partridge, blancmange, ducks, plum pudding, goose and apple sauce! For the third course there were 'plenty of apples, raisins, nuts, olives, bread, butter and cheese, as well as celery left over from the second course'.

The **St Andrew Society, Albuquerque**, New Mexico has a membership of 200 families. Their largest gathering is for the Robert Burns Night, which is well attended by non-members. The St Andrew Night is celebrated with a Dinner or Pot-Luck Supper – pipers and drummers sometimes play on these occasions. Many years ago, members looked forward to the box of heather that Scottish school-children picked and boxed and sent overseas to them. It was always a thrill to receive this gift, but the postage became so high that it had to be stopped.

Highland Games are held in May when there are dog-herding demonstrations, rugby tournaments, Highland Dance competitions, and pipe and drum competitions. Traditionally another British society, the Daughters of the British Empire, organise the tea tent for which they bake Scottish shortbread.

The **St Andrew Scottish Society of New Mexico** publishes a newsletter whose title is *The Thistle Epistle*. The cosmopolitan nature of ex-patriot associations can be seen in the activities shared with other national societies – a Ceilidh with the Irish-American Society; or a Pot-Luck supper at the German-American Club.

Organised in 1863, during the colourful days of California's Gold Rush, the **St Andrew Society of San Francisco** was formed by a group of Scotsmen anxious to preserve and further their own traditions and culture and to aid Scots in distress. The Society brought together those who longed to hear their own speech, the skirl of the bagpipe, and the music and poetry of the Scotland they had left.

Today, aid to people in distress of Scots origin or descent remains an important function for the Society, whose Board of Student Assistance, for example, helps students who are from Northern California or from Scotland.

In terms of cultural promotion, encouragement in tangible form is given to bagpipe bands, Highland dance groups, and Celtic music study. The Society's 'Hospitality Tent' is a feature of Highland Games held across Northern California.

The **St Andrew's Society of the Eastern Shore** is so named because most of its members reside on the eastern shore of the Chesapeake Bay, an area comprising portions of three states –

Delaware, Maryland and Virginia (the so-called DelMarVa Peninsula).

Membership is available to both men and women of Scottish birth or ancestry. The Society provides charitable and educational assistance to Scottish men and women, their descendants and their widows or widowers.

To help promote and perpetuate Scottish traditions and culture, the Society sponsors instruction in pipes, drums and Scottish country dancing. Its social activities include meetings, luncheons, dinners, picnics and ceilidhs. The Society is not affiliated to any secular or religious organisation.

Each November, members celebrate the birth of St Andrew by sponsoring a dinner in his honour, at which time their newly-elected officers and directors are installed.

In summer 1995, with the help of financial grants from the Society, two young ladies from the area visited Scotland. One was participating in the 'People to People' program; the other conducting an archaeological dig in northwest Scotland.

In the northeast of America, on 6 January 1657, only twenty years after the founding of the city, the **Scots Charitable Society of Boston** was organised for the relief of Scots. Almost a century later in 1749, the **Saint Andrew's Society of Philadelphia** was founded by 25 Scottish residents to give relief to the poor and the distressed. Two signatories of the Declaration of Independence – James Wilson (a graduate of St Andrews University) and John Witherspoon DD, a native of Paisley and president of Princeton College – were founder members.

Nearly ten years later, in 1756, the **Saint Andrew's Society of the State of New York** was founded as a charitable organisation. Colonel Simon Fraser, the eldest son of Lord Lovat, was a member.

The Society has a membership today of close to one thousand men. The Society holds an annual banquet at the Waldorf-Astoria hotel with two guest speakers on the topics 'The Land we live in' and 'The Land o' Cakes'. In 1994 the speaker on the latter theme was Lord Younger of Prestwick. The evening's entertainment is provided by two pipe bands, herald trumpeters, the singing of Scottish songs, and a haggis ceremony.

In 1994 the bill of fare consisted of cock-a-leekie soup, haggis, mashed turnips and oat cakes. This was followed by sirloin of beef, roast potatoes, glazed baby carrots and sautéed zucchini, finishing with shortbread and a choice of wine or whisky. Pipes and drums, the presentation of colours and Scots songs enlivened the proceedings.

Present were representatives from many societies including the Sons of the American Revolution, the Society of Colonial Wars, and Scottish Heritage USA, Inc.

The **North British Society** in Halifax, Nova Scotia was founded in 1768 and (outside Great Britain) is said to be the oldest Scottish heritage society in the Commonwealth, being open to persons of Scottish relationship by descent, marriage or affiliation. In its very first year, the founders 'unanimously agreed that the annual feast of this Society be held on St Andrew's Day'. The founders' decision has been observed ever since, with certain particular exceptions – for instance, during the years of World War.

The Society's historian and past president, Donald F Maclean, writes:

> *When we toast St Andrew we have a sense of honouring Scotland, our own Scottish antecedents and heritage. Perhaps we do not have quite so strong a sense of honouring a religious figure. St Andrew may have come to be, for us, primarily a symbol of patriotism. But our Nova Scotia flag [the flag of Scotland with colours reversed], is a constant reminder, at least subconsciously, of St Andrew.*

Nineteen years after the founding of Halifax (1749), and five years before the arrival of the ship 'Hector' in 1773 which marked the beginning of mainstream Scottish emigration to Nova Scotia, a small group of Scots immigrants met in Halifax to organise the North British Society.

According to the literature of the Society, use of the term 'Great Britain' instead of 'Scotland' was characteristic of the eighteenth century Enlightenment's ardent belief that eventually there would be achieved a common and vital *British* culture. The expression 'North Britain' did not imply, in the eighteenth century, any notion that Scotland was a secondary or subordinate adjunct to a larger power.

Poignantly aware that 'sickness and death are the common lot of all mankind', the group resolved to bind themselves into a Society 'for the benefit of ourselves and assistance of each other, who may be afflicted with disease or any other casualty or misfortune'.

Through the years, the Society has extended financial assistance to persons and families in need, to destitute widows, to shipwrecked mariners, and worked for the return of elderly persons to their homes in Scotland.

Public gifts by the Society have included a statue of Robert Burns, a bust of Sir Walter Scott, the Robert Stevenson Memorial Library, and the presentation of microfiche copies of the surviving parish records (1553-1854) of the Church of Scotland. In recent years the Society has organised the Metropolitan Festival and Highland Games, a showcase for promoting the image and raison d'être of the Society.

The **St Andrew's Society of Washington** honours St Andrew as part of their annual 'Kirkin' o' the Tartan' at the National Cathedral each April. They also honour him in one of the toasts at the annual 'Burns Nicht' Dinner.

In his Toast to St Andrew, Jim MacGregor cleverly made the connection between St Andrew and the character traditionally attributed to the Scot:

> *They say a Scot is thrifty. St Andrew lived with his brother and the family. Maybe he did so because he was single. On the other hand, maybe he was saving his pennies.*
>
> *A Scot is thought to have an independent spirit – not bound by tradition. We know that Andrew was a follower of John the Baptist who preached against the establishment and its traditions. John was not a popular figure among the ruling class.*
>
> *We Scots are said to have an open mind and to value learning. Andrew sought an interview with the Lord to hear the gospel message first-hand. He had to determine for himself whether or not to follow Him.*
>
> *They say a Scot has enthusiasm and the courage of his convictions. Andrew believed the Lord. He went to his brother Peter and told him he had found the Messiah. He introduced Peter to the Lord. Could it be said that St Andrew was the first domestic missionary?*
>
> *We all know a Scot has reserve. Andrew was one of the first four Apostles. He is always mentioned with, but less frequently than, the other three. Maybe he was not part of the 'inner circle' – or perhaps he was and just did not blether about it.*
>
> *Scots are said to have a metaphysical bent. Andrew was one of those who inquired of the Lord about the signs of the end times.*
>
> *A Scot is practical, a man of action. Andrew heard the discussion of how to feed the thousands of people. He found the boy with the five barley loaves and two fish. He directed the people to be seated. Maybe he also supervised the distribution.*
>
> *A Scot can be a devoted, dutiful servant. The Greeks wanted an interview with the Lord. They asked Philip. Andrew took the request to the Lord. Could St Andrew have been the first missionary to foreigners?*
>
> *A Scot is loyal. Andrew was with the others in the upper room in the*

scary time after the Lord's resurrection. St Andrew is a true role model for us Scots!

Founded in 1806, the **St Andrew's Society of Baltimore** takes part in an annual 'Kirkin' of the Tartans' ceremony. With the Kiltie Band, about 35 men in Highland day-wear parade along the streets of Baltimore for four blocks before marching into church. During the service, which is dedicated to St Andrew, the tartans of the clans of Scotland are piped to the altar and blessed.

After the congregation sings the 'Old Hundredth', the tartans are presented with the following prayer:

God of our fathers and mothers and of the long line of brave and good people who brought honour to Scotland by keeping the light of faith and patriotism in dark days, who surrounded hardships and sorrow with skirling pipes and the colours of unconquerable clans, and who celebrated life with dance and song and your gift of Highland dew; We, the descendants, now bring before you these tartans, symbols of our families past and present. We ask your blessing on them and all that they stand for; that we, in our generation, may pass on to others the spiritual greatness that we have received, for the honour of your Name and for the well-being of all mankind. In the name of Andrew the Apostle and Patron Saint of Scotland, and of Jesus Christ our Lord.

Every year the Society holds a large banquet in honour of St Andrew attended by about 450 men. After grace, and toasts to the President of the United States and to Scotia, the Haggis is addressed. Speeches are interwoven with piping and the music of the pipes and drums before the evening ends with the singing of 'Auld Lang Syne'.

First organised in 1803, the **St Andrew's Society, Albany** in New York has a membership today of around 125 men. Significantly, the Society's growth in numbers has been due to the interest of younger men in their Scottish heritage. Some of the more active, younger members are native Scots who have come over in the past decade. The work of the Society is of a charitable nature.

Born out of concern and love for fellow countrymen on 8 February 1802, the St Andrew's Society began as the United Irish and Scotch Benevolent Society. A year later this group was dissolved and out of it 18 men of Scottish birth founded the St Andrew's Society at Tontines Coffee House on 7 October 1803.

The early days of the Society were filled with the activity of aiding the many Scots arriving from Scotland. Over the years, the Society has given a considerable amount of money as gifts, grants and loans to individuals, worthy charities, civic organisations and Scottish causes.

Among the distinguished Scots who have been members are Joseph Henry, founder of the United States national weather service, secretary of the Smithsonian Institution, and discoverer of electrical magnetism. Another was the industrialist Andrew Carnegie.

The Society meets five times a year at the Rooms, a historic three-storey building which contains a main meeting room, decorated with Clan shields, a baronial fireplace, and many Scottish artefacts. Other features include a Wee Kitchen, an extensive library and a large garden.

St Andrew's Day is the highlight of the Society's year, consisting (in 1994) of Cameronian Haggis, Cock-a-Leekie Soup and Inverewe Salad. Then a choice of Prime Ribs of Glaswegian Beef, Breast of Spey Valley Chicken, or Broiled Aberdeen Haddock. Lastly on 'St Andrew's Nicht', excerpts from Wallace Bruce's *St Andrew's Sons* are recited:

A miracle of truth divine,
A martyr's cross, a hallowed shrine ...
The martyr's lips at Patras stilled,
The Scottish heart with triumph thrilled.

Founded in 1923, the object of the **Saint Andrew's Society of Rhode Island** is to foster interest in and to promote the study of Scottish folklore, history, literature and tradition, by providing opportunities for the presentation and discussion of subjects of interest to its members; to promote social activities and to support charitable enterprises as financially feasible; and to further any desirable or deserving Scottish movement as so directed by the officers and executive committee.

The Society holds its St Andrew's Day celebration in mid-November to avoid conflict with Thanksgiving (last Thursday in November). There is a 'Kirking of the Tartans' on the Sunday closest to Veterans Day (11 November): 'We always place a wee bit of tartan ribbon on the church program so that we can take it and stick it on one's clothing and become Scottish for an hour or so.'

The following Saturday a dinner-dance is held, buffet-style, complete with the Haggis Ceremony, Scottish music and country dancing. Some members are also vendors of Scottish goods and apparel. They take annual turns displaying their wares and ten percent of their profit is donated to the St Andrew's Society of Rhode Island Scholarship Fund, Inc.

Membership is made up not only of adult men and women, but also of children and grandchildren, for whom there is a children's story-telling party at a date after the dinner dance and before Thanksgiving. The service itself includes a reading of *Psalm 23* in Scots translated by Society member Neil Sharpe:

The Laird's my Herd, I sallnae want;
He loots me to lie doon,
At owre the knowes, an' in green howes,
Whaur bonnie burnies croon.
My saul He waukins frae its dwam,
Oot o' the muirlands weet,
Intil richt roads – for His Name's sake –
He airts my wann'ring feet.
Nu, to' I hae to gang my lane,
Doon through the deid mirk dale,
I'll thole nae skaith, for ye are bye,
Your crook an' kent ne'er fail.
My grainin' buird ye've hanselit, while
My faes did sit and' glower;
My pow wi' Ile is dreepin wat,
My bicker's lippin ower.
Guid guidin' an guid greenin' sall
Gang wi' me late an' air;
An' syne up i' the Laird's big hoose
I'll bide for ever mair.

According to one of the programs of the Society, the 'Kirking of the Tartans' recalls that 'for Highland clansmen, the tartan signified a covenantal relationship between God and each family of believers'. It is also a 'remembrance of the Patron Saint of Scotland and a celebration of heritage and rededication to the service of God'.

In Canada, the **Saint Andrew's Society of Montreal** was established in 1835, setting up the Saint Andrew's Home and other direct charitable agencies. The **Saint Andrew's Society of Toronto** followed a year later. The **London, Ontario St Andrew's and Caledonian Society** appeared around 1875.

As one contemporary publication put it: 'By most of these societies the 30th day of November in each year is observed as a time of great rejoicing. Then the patriotism of the members is freely expressed, and they extol their native land, its hills and valleys and streams, its men and women, its history, its battles, its antiquities, its discoveries.'

Founded in 1835, the principal aims of the Saint Andrew's Society of Montreal are to sustain, assist and encourage those less fortunate kith of Scottish birth or descent; to provide youth of Scottish ancestry in the Province of Quebec with opportunities to advance their education through bursaries, scholarships and loans; to maintain and preserve Scottish traditions in the community by promoting historical, cultural, patriotic, social and sporting activities.

The first Scots to celebrate St Andrew's Day in Montreal may have been those who served with the Chevalier James de Johnstone in the army of Louis X. The Scots fighting for George III certainly did so.

The first recorded St Andrew's Ball was held on 2 December 1816. The *Montreal Herald* describes the scene:

> *The dancing commenced about seven o'clock and continued with great spirit till after midnight, when the company to the number of about 130, sat down to a sumptuous and elegant supper .... The supper room was handsomely decorated, having at the upper end a transparency of glass lit behind by candles representing St Andrew at full length.*
>
> *Suppers were lavish: a pyramid of quail, a suckling pig à l'Italienne and a boar's head. The entry of the haggis was a central feature. After supper the dancing continued with much vivacity till five o'clock.*

The primary function of the Society in its earliest years was to administer charity from funds collected. In 1852, travel expenses of £94 were given to immigrants; some £372 was given to the families of those killed in the Crimean War; £263 was given to local charities.

The first of a series of St Andrew's Homes for the accommodation of immigrants was rented in 1857. When a disastrous fire broke out on the 'SS Montreal', 254 people were killed. Of the passengers, 320 were Scottish immigrants and 76 survivors were cared for in the new Home. The Committee arranged for the identification and burial of the dead, and the disposition of their clothing and belongings. In the pocket of one of the victims was found a stanza of *The Exile's Song:*

> *Oh! Why left I my hame,*
> *Why did I cross the deep?*
> *Oh! Why left I the land*

Where my forfathers sleep?
I sigh for Scotia's shore,
And I gaze across the sea:
But I canna get a blink
O' my ain countrie!

Since its inception the Society has taken pride in its members as builders of Canada. In 1858 a bill was enacted to broaden the Society's powers, enabling it to carry out welfare and youth-training activities among those of Scottish birth or descent, as well as social, artistic and sporting activities for the purpose of maintaining Scottish traditions. In 1972, over $17,000 was spent on welfare and education grants.

Singapore St Andrew's Society, founded around 1836, celebrates with an annual Ball with some 400 people present. In addition to flying in a guest speaker, the Society provides a Scottish band and a piper. Normally there is an exhibition dance by the Society's Country Dance team, along with performances by the Royal Gurkhas. Athol Brose is served before dinner.

In 1994 the dinner consisted of cock-a-leekie soup, haggis, turnip and potatoes, Scottish salmon, a sweet (Blairgowrie Delight) and cheese and oatcakes.

Australians Ross and Kathy Taylor gave a personal reaction to the ceremonies in the Society's newsletter:

'Ok, yeah, sure we'd like to come,' was our innocent response to the invitation to go to the 1994 St Andrew's Ball. 'Before we knew it we were being embroiled in all types of odd Scottish traditions. Whoever heard of a Ball that you practise for? We didn't think they could possibly be serious.

'In no time, we were having explained to us what sets, poosets and strathspeys were. (We had always thought a strathspey was an Aussie cat, but you live and learn). We were then asked to put these strange terms into practice, while simultaneously trying to remember the actual dance sequence, keep in time with the music, and concentrate on the different instructions that seemed to be flooding in from all directions.

'To our surprise, however, over the six weeks prior to the Ball, we found ourselves making tangible progress and actually enjoying ourselves.

'By the time the night of the Ball was upon us, we found ourselves regretting we weren't Scottish with a long history of dancing, kilt-wearing and bagpipe-blowing.

'When you get inside the main reception room at the Shangri-la Hotel you find it's as if you have been beamed up out of Singapore to somewhere *in the Scottish Highlands. It seemed that tartan and kilts were taking over the world.*

'In the ballroom we learnt our first Scottish phrase: "Lang may yer lum reek! – ye cowrin' timrous beastie."

'The bagpipes started to honour the entry of the Haggis. Who would have thought someone would fly a bag of entrails half-way around the world, honour its entry to a Ball with bagpipes, drums and 600 people standing, arrange for it to be greeted ceremoniously by a Chieftain and finally have it served up with silver service and laced with 12-year old Scotch whisky?'

The **Belfast Benevolent Society of St Andrew** has been in continuous operation since its foundation in 1867 and members have held a St Andrew's Day Dinner each year, with the exception of two years in the First World War. In November 1810, the following appeared in the Belfast newsletter:

The Festival of St Andrew, the Tutelar Saint of Scotland, will be celebrated at the Donegall Arms on Friday, 30 November 1810. Dinner on the table at five o'clock. The stewards give this general invitation to all Scotch Gentlemen who may find it convenient to attend and they require the honour of the Company of such Irish Gentlemen as incline to be of the party. Tickets three crowns each.

The Society was founded through the efforts of David Taylor of Perth and John Arnott from Auchtermuchty, who had arrived in Belfast in the early 1860s. Together they founded Arnott's Stores. John Arnott later became Mayor of Cork and David Taylor was elected Mayor of Belfast. Both were subsequently knighted.

The aims of the Society were to alleviate distress among Scots and their dependants; to assist charitable objectives; and to afford opportunity for social meetings. However, it was hoped that the new Society would 'be the means of bringing together in closer communion Scots who, while cherishing a lively regard for the country they live in, are yet desirous of showing they do not forget the land which gave them birth'. There was a caveat:

It is not, however, a Society for the encouragement of mutual esteem, or for the fostering of that sort of nationalism which loves to dwell on the meaner and provincial attributes of a country, or at best to elevate it to the comparative detriment of another.

In the Far East, the **Saint Andrew's Society of Kobe**, Japan holds a spring and an autumn ceilidh. Members also have a Burns Supper and the St Andrew's Ball. The AGM is held in April, usually followed by another ceilidh. The ceilidhs normally attract about fifty people, both Japanese and Scottish. There are normally about one hundred attending the Ball. The Society is open to all-comers, but the committee members must have Scottish blood.

In Africa, the **Harare Caledonian Society of Zimbabwe** usually celebrates St Andrew's Day annually with a dinner-dance. The emphasis that evening is on St Andrew. During the course of the night, two speakers are invited to address the gathering. The main topic is 'St Andrew and Bonnie Scotland' and the speaker is invited to discourse for about 15 minutes, after which those present are invited to drink a toast to St Andrew. The second speaker's topic is 'The Land we live in' – probably appropriate for those members who are exiled Scots, living permanently in Zimbabwe.

The **St Andrew's Society of the River Plate** in Buenos Aires, Argentina is a flourishing one. The nearest Sunday to 30 November, the members celebrate a St Andrew's Day Service at the St Andrew's Presbyterian City Church, with the attendance of people from the British Embassy and some other special guests. The Pipe Band of the Society plays at the service.

On the Saturday before the Service, members organise the St Andrew's Day Banquet which is held at the English Club. There, beside the performance of the Pipe Band and Highland Dancers, members parade with the banners of the Clans of members of the Society, eat haggis, and dance Scottish country dances.

Founded in 1895, the **St Andrew's Society of Uruguay** annually celebrates St Andrew's Day at the residence of the British Ambassador, with a dinner to which guests are invited to attend in highland dress, dinner jackets or dark suits.

Normally there are over eighty persons present for the four-course dinner, including haggis which is brought in ceremoniously accompanied by two pipers. Speeches are followed by toasts to 'The Land in which we live', 'Bonnie Scotland', 'The Lassies' and a 'Reply from the Lassies'. After dinner there is Scottish country dancing.

President Martin Fraser Gibson comments that 'St Andrew as the Patron Saint of Scotland is part of our Scottish heritage and is the instigator of all our Scottish traditions and events'.

Moving across the Pacific to New Zealand, the **City of Napier Caledonian Society** celebrates St Andrew's Day on the Sunday nearest the 30 November. The Pipe Band and the Scottish Country Dancers combine for a 'Kirkin' of the Tartan' at St Paul's Presbyterian Church. This is preceded by a march to the Church with tartan banners proudly displayed. During the service, everyone present is invited to present their own tartan for blessing. The readings are done by representatives of Scottish organisations.

The second event on the 30 November is a ceilidh involving all Scottish organisations – Scottish societies, pipe bands, Highland dancers and Scottish country dancers in the district.

Although many members are third and even fourth generation New Zealanders, they greatly value their links with Scotland, the land of their forebears, and they honour its patron saint, Andrew. Members feel, however, that to many people, St Andrew is just a name. The Society intends to redress this anomaly. Typical of the depth of feeling experienced by members is the sermon delivered by the Revd Colin English on 29 November 1992 at St Paul's Presbyterian Church, Napier:

> *Nationalism, pride in our nation, in one's social and cultural roots, in one's religious roots, is something to be welcomed when it enhances and enriches the life of the human family and our national family.*
>
> *Martin Niemöller is a potent reminder of the fallacy of compartmentalizing our lives on the basis of our own self-identity. Equally, distinctions can enrich and enhance the life of any community when we allow them. Nationalism and pride in our race and culture is good when it unites and bad when it divides. It is good when it gives me pride in my background and helps me to appreciate the background of others. It is bad, even idolatrous, when it cuts me off from others because they are 'different' from me, whether in religion, race or creed. It is bad when I feel no responsibility for others because they are identified by a label different from my own.*

In nearby Australia, the **Melbourne Scots** were founded in 1919. The Society is open to men of Scottish birth or descent, but has a 'no publicity' rule and functions are communicated only to members. 'We have found this policy to operate well,' writes honorary secretary, John G Cooper, 'especially as many of our members and guests are "newsworthy". We therefore offer them freedom from press photography and reporting when they attend activities of the Society.'

Membership is limited to 240 and, as vacancies arise, they are filled from the waiting list. Currently it takes around four years between going on the waiting list and admission.

The main activity of the Society is a formal dinner. The Society has a strong Banffshire/Aberdeenshire contingent within the membership and appreciates the Doric language in the dinner menu – 'Haggis an' Atholl Brose; Hoch o' Hoggie wi' a jilp o' mushroom bree; followed by Crumlie Kebbuck.'

The Grace before dinner sums up the ethos of the Society: 'For a goodly heritage, for proud traditions and cherished memories, for good fellowship and good fare, we give Thee thanks, O Lord and crave Thy blessing.'

Moving north, the **Hong Kong St Andrew's Society** celebrates St Andrew's Day with a St Andrew's Ball attended by some six hundred people, including guests from the St George, St David and St Patrick Societies. At the ball a toast is given to St Andrew, with reference to the biblical origins of the saint. It is an opportunity to gather together as Scots.

As well as a church service, the St Andrew's Quaich is competed for at a horse race meeting, the St Andrew's team competes against the St George's team at rugby, and there is a wreath-laying ceremony at which respects are paid to compatriots who lost their lives in battle.

The **Selangor (Kuala Lumpur) St Andrew's Society** was established in 1887 and today has around one hundred members, only half to three-quarters being born and brought up in Scotland. Other members are of Scottish descent

The major social event of the year is the annual Ball to which members can invite guests. After the speeches and toasts during the first half of the evening, almost everyone takes part in the Scottish dancing which has been faithfully practised by members and guests alike for weeks beforehand.

A programme note on the annual celebration menu-card records that St Andrew apparently first brought Christianity to the Romanians, where superstition has it that ghosts and werewolves roam on St Andrew's Day. '[In 1993],' continues the note, 'in Romania, a rural publication, *Evenimentul Ziliei,* urged Romanians to consume large quantities of garlic and to rub it on the windows and doors of their homes to ward off werewolves, vampires and other malevolent spirits on St Andrew's Day.'

Beginning with the 'Selkirk Grace', the meal in 1994 consisted of Scotch salmon rose, garnished with assorted lettuce and asparagus bouquet, served with balsamic vinaigrette. This was followed by haggis, neeps and tatties; Lamb *persillade à l'Écosse* with rosemary sauce, served with carrot flan; a spiced flummery and Boh coffee or

Boh tea. The occasion was decorated with white heather, flags, banners, Bruce and Wallace shields, and a ram's head.

When dancing commenced, these included eightsome reels, a piping display, the Dashing White Sergeant and Strip the Willow.

Back in Europe, in Scandinavia, a unique and honourable history is attached to the **Caledonian Society of Norway** (patron, the Duke of Argyle).

During the period immediately after the Second World War, when a wave of spontaneous rejoicing flooded over Norway, many Allied soldiers took an active and very welcome part in Norwegian social life. Among them was Sergeant-Major James W Blair.

The evening of his arrival in Oslo, Sergeant-Major Blair went for a stroll up the hill in the direction of the Royal Palace. There he encountered a Norwegian who was on his way down the hill to the main street of Oslo, Karl Johan, a popular meeting-place at that time of public rejoicing. The Norwegian was Willy Sommerfeldt Jacobsen. He and the Scottish soldier got into a conversation. This was the casual beginning to what would later develop into a warm friendship and mutual respect.

One day, James Blair suggested to Willy Sommerfeldt that they should start a Scottish-Norwegian society. By this time the Scot had made a large number of Norwegian friends.

On Wednesday 11 September 1946, James Blair invited two fellow-Scots and three Norwegians to No. 862 – his room at the Hotel Continental – which was at that time reserved for Allied forces. Then he put to them his idea of forming a Scottish-Norwegian society.

A temporary committee was established and given the task of drawing up a constitution and enrolling members. On the committee was J Solheim, a journalist on the *Morgenbladet*. He had previously been in touch with James Blair when preparing an article on the Scots. He became the founder-member and secretary.

James Blair was recalled to Scotland in the autumn of 1946, leaving Norway for good. However, the seed had been sown and by the following year there were 16 members of the new Caledonian Society of Norway. The aim of the Society was to form a cultural and intimate relationship between the two countries. Although this rather ambitious goal has not been met fully, the Society has been a valuable link in the chain binding the two nations together.

The two major functions in the Society's year were St Andrew's Night and Burns' Night. At the monthly meetings at the Villa Granberg, lectures, films and other entertainment were provided. In later years, meeting were held in Rune's Skipperstue or at Det norske Medicinske Selskab. A St Andrew's Ball was a popular feature. Guests were welcomed with flaring torches in the dark winter evenings. They walked up the steps of the Villa Granberg on a red carpet, to be met by trumpet fanfares.

Dress at the ball (now sadly, due to rising costs, no longer an annual event) was Full Highland Dress or white tie, with ladies in all their finery. Sometimes a pantomime, based on historical events precedes dinner. These have included King James VI of Scotland with his bride, Princess Anne of Norway.

After cocktails and dinner, the Grand March and Ball began. On several occasions a piper was imported from Scotland or from a Scottish regiment serving in Germany. Eightsome reels were always danced and the evening ends with 'Auld Lang Syne'.

Wreaths have also been placed at the unveiling of the monument commemorating British servicemen who fell in Norway during the Second World War.

During the Kalmar War (1611-13) between Sweden and Denmark/Norway, three hundred Scottish mercenary soldiers were hired by the Swedish King Charles IX and placed under the command of Lieutenant Colonel Alexander Ramsay. They were ordered to fight their way through Norway to join the king in Sweden.

The Scots landed at Romsdalsfjorden on 21 August 1612 and began to march up the valleys. However, at Kringen, the local farmers assembled to prevent them passing. The farmers prepared an avalanche of wood and boulders and when a company led by Captain George Sinclair passed on the morning of 26 August, the avalanche was released and the Scots came under heavy fire. Many died. The Norwegians took 134 prisoners, of whom only 18 survived.

During the Second World War, 50 British soldiers were killed in the same area. On 26 August 1962, some 12,000 people assembled to commemorate these events.

In 1981 the Society was instrumental in forming the Oslo Scottish Country Dancing Group, affiliated to the Royal Scottish Country Dance Society. The Caledonian Society also provides tickets for members wishing to attend international football matches between Scotland and Norway at the Ullevål Stadion. At these matches, the Society's piper had led the Scots team onto the field.

Chapter 12

SAINT ANDREW
AND MODERN
SCOTLAND

Public Holiday

WHILE there can be no doubt about the historical importance of St Andrew as a symbol of Scottish identity, the logical step of declaring 30 November a Public or a Bank Holiday is not universally accepted as desirable.

There are many who are convinced of the need to declare St Andrew's Day a Public Holiday. Former City of Edinburgh District Councillor Devin Scobie (Scottish Liberal Democrat Recreation and Tourism Spokesman) waged a personal campaign in favour of a Public Holiday within Scotland on St Andrew's Day – what Councillor Scobie describes as his 'mini-crusade':

> *Scotland has fewer recognised Public Holidays than the rest of the United Kingdom. We have none which mark or remember any part of our history or culture.*
>
> *Conversely, many towns and cities in Scotland have a bewildering variety of local and business holidays which few people really understand. If the Secretary of State does not support a St Andrew's Day Holiday, I would like to see the City of Edinburgh take the lead and replace one of its Spring local holidays with a St Andrew's Day holiday, perhaps on the Monday closest to 30 November.*
>
> *Our patron saint has gone without recognition for centuries. As we approach the new millennium, I would like to see the year 2000 as a target date for the new St Andrew's Day Holiday to be in place.*

Of the Scottish MPs circularised by Councillor Scobie on 15 July 1994, some 26 were in favour of making 30 November a Public Holiday; nine were opposed the idea and six refused to express an opinion. The number of Scottish MPs who favoured the proposal were: Labour (20 out of 47); Conservative (9 out of 10); Liberal Democrat (8 out of 9); Scottish National Party (3 out of 3).

The SNP's Andrew Welsh MP tabled an Early Day motion in the House of Commons on 29 November 1994, calling for the adoption of St Andrew's Day as a Public Holiday in Scotland. He said:

> It is an anomaly that the day celebrating Scotland's patron saint is not a Public Holiday in Scotland. Throughout Europe other countries have the day of their patron saint as an official Public Holiday. In comparison, Scotland has less Public Holidays than these other European countries. It is now time for the Government to make Saint Andrew's Day an official Public Holiday and to mark the day by encouraging the flying of the cross of Saint Andrew.

On 21 July 1995, Robert Maclennan, Liberal Democrat MP for Caithness and Sutherland, responding to Councillor Scobie, tabled a Parliamentary Question to the Secretary of State: 'If he will consider the designation of St Andrew's Day as a Public Holiday in Scotland.'

Replying on behalf of the Secretary of State for Scotland, Lord James Douglas-Hamilton, in a written answer, said: 'Public holidays in Scotland are not defined in statute, but by long tradition and practice are determined by individual local authorities in consultation with local interests. My Right Honourable Friend has no power to intervene in this process.'

In a letter to Robert Maclennan MP on 30 November 1994, the Minister for Home Affairs and Health, Lord Fraser of Carmyllie QC, pointed out:

> It is open to any authority to declare St Andrew's Day as a holiday; that none has apparently done so suggests that a holiday at the end of November may not be particularly attractive to many people.

He concluded:

> The Secretary of State has no power to intervene in the process of determining local Public Holidays and, given the limited significance of bank holidays in Scotland generally and the lack of public interest, the Government see no need to designate an additional Bank Holiday for St Andrew's Day'.

It is, however, clear that the Secretary of State would have the power to designate St Andrew's Day as a Bank Holiday. Paragraph 2 of

Schedule 1 of the Banking and Financial Dealing Act 1971 designates the following days as Bank Holidays in Scotland:

- New Year's Day (if it be not a Sunday);
- or (if it be a Sunday) 3rd January;
- 2nd January (if it be not a Sunday);
- or (if it be a Sunday), 3rd January;
- Good Friday;
- the first Monday in May;
- the first Monday in August.

Section 1(92) of the Act gives the Queen the power to change the days set out in Schedule 1 by Royal Proclamation; and Section 1(93) gives her the power to appoint any other days as a Bank Holiday by Royal Proclamation.

There appears to be no reason why the Secretary of State for Scotland could not ask the Queen to declare St Andrew's Day (30 November) a Bank Holiday, by Royal Proclamation under Section 1(93) of the Act. It might be that people in some places in Scotland would continue to treat it as a normal working day, but that others might treat it as a Public Holiday.

Writing in *The Herald* on 1 December 1994, the Scottish National Party's Alex Salmond argued forcefully for a Public Holiday on 30 November:

> *While other countries celebrate their national day in style, St Andrew is relegated to B-league status in his adopted homeland. Compared to the two other Scottish festivals – Burns Night and Hogmanay – the feast day of Andrew hardly gets a look in.*
>
> *I'm in favour of a national holiday for St Andrew's Day and the full works in terms of school projects, national competitions, sporting and cultural events .... A proper remembrance of St Andrew would give us all the opportunity to reflect on our national shortage of self worth and help give us the determination to change things for the better.*

And, in an article published in *Flourish*, the newspaper of the Roman Catholic Archdiocese of Glasgow, Mr Salmond added:

> *Andrew the man knew the importance of hard work and the importance of working as a team for mutual benefit. He was a working fisherman, without education, but still chosen to provide leadership at a critical moment.*

He could still be an inspirational figure to the country which had the privilege of adopting his cross. A Public Holiday on St Andrew's Day could be an effective way of remembering some lessons about the simplicity of our roots and making some private vows about the need to work together to build a country more worthy of its patron saint.

Perceptively, novelist and commentator Allan Massie observed in *Scotland on Sunday* (27 November 1994): '... the first significance of Scotland's adoption of St Andrew as patron saint was that it put us at the heart of Europe.'

Commercial Aspects

Teasing out the commercial implications of making 30 November a Public Holiday, presenter Chris Mann looked at the arguments for and against on 30 November 1994, in company with a number of interested parties on Radio Scot-FM.

Public Relations Director of the Scottish Tourist Board, Graham Birse, began by remembering:

St Andrew really helped shape the nation of Scotland. We are told that in AD 735 there was a battle at Athelstaneford in East Lothian and afterwards St Andrew was declared to be the patron saint of Alba – what is now Scotland. So, in a sense, he is our patron saint and St Andrews in Fife, of course is not merely associated with golf. It's associated with his name.

It is something of a paradox that we celebrate St Andrew in our saltire cross and that throughout the world there are St Andrew societies from Hong Kong to San Francisco who, on 30 November, hold great celebrations in his name – it's become a celebration of their Scottishness because they're so far from home – yet, there isn't a holiday here in Scotland and we don't make a great fuss about it.

The Scottish Tourist Board would like to see a Public Holiday, although I would stress that I don't think that those of us who work in Tourism should take a holiday on that particular day – we should be taking advantage of it.

From overseas, there's this great interest in Scottish images and Scottish culture. The other day, at the consul-general's residence in Milan, the Scottish Tourist Board held a St Andrew's Night dinner for journalists and for travel trade representatives and we had traditional Scottish entertain-

ment. We tried to do it in a quality way – it wasn't a 'teuchter' night, but there was great appetite and interest in all the imagery associated with it. Our tourist industry is, after all, our largest industry now. It's worth £2 billion and 185,000 jobs depend on it. We really ought to be doing as much as we can to present our image to the world and encourage that trade.

Here in Scotland, perhaps we could do more in an educational sense about St Andrew. We could, perhaps, do more interpretation about the places his remains visited. St Andrews is an obvious place for an interpretation centre, for example.

I know that the Saltire flies proudly at Athelstaneford in East Lothian. Perhaps another interpretation could be introduced; more events, more pageantry, more celebration.

I think it's certainly true to say that there is a case for more economic development associated with a Public Holiday – that's associated with tourism. If we declared a Public Holiday on St Andrew's Day then I think a great deal of benefit could accrue to the tourist business, not just at a local, but at a national level. I am prepared to accept that it could provide a disruption elsewhere and I think the best solution would be to supplant one of the other Public Holidays (many of which are meaningless, as far as our national heritage goes), with St Andrew's Day. It would be very useful to have a day's holiday at this time of year, because St Andrew's Day, from the tourist point of view, happily falls outside the main tourist season. We're seeking to push the season and extend it. It would also be useful for Scots to have a nice early holiday before Christmas to get the shopping done.

Ian Brown of the Edinburgh Chamber of Commerce was equally supportive:

I've no doubt at all that the greater use of the saltire in trying to sell Scottish business would be highly beneficial. Before I came to the Chamber of Commerce, I spent eight years travelling Europe and the world, promoting Scottish food products. I've got no doubt whatsoever that the Scottish image is very, very strong abroad and anything we can do to strengthen that would only be beneficial.

I think that there's a considerable recognition that the saltire represents Scotland. The more that's done to use it and promote it, the better.

This brought the rejoinder from Graham Birse:

In fact, tartan is more likely to be recognised overseas than the saltire. We're involved, along with other commercial partners, in a project called 'Scotland the Brand' which is about presenting Scotland and Scottish products associated with the environment and the heritage and the quality of knitwear, textiles, whisky, tourism, beef, lamb. That essentially was our message in Milan, but presented (wrapped around, if you like) in a Scottish Heritage package which is extremely attractive and desirable. We need to do more of that in order to develop a recognition and in order to introduce the saltire more frequently to our overseas customers. This does not have to be a nationalistic feeling – in terms of Scottish independence or separation; it communicates that we have sets of products and services that are unique to Scotland and have a premium, a quality associated with them that we're seeking to sell'.

Added Mr Birse:

I do think that, in association with St Andrew, there is an opportunity overseas to develop links; to use – or perhaps, to work alongside the St Andrew's societies and the exiled Scots, most of whom (in fact, all of whom, in my experience) are fiercely patriotic, want to contribute something back to the Old Country. Those people, I think, would be very prepared to act as our envoys in the absence of a traditional network.

Rounding off the discussion, Ian Brown concluded:

There's no doubt about it that a Scottish network exists abroad and could be used. We really ought to capitalise on the ex-pat Scots living abroad to do the very best for us – to promote the country and its products. I think there is another point as well. There's a limit to how far we really ought to take the 'haggis and tartan' image. Okay, it has a limited appeal, but I think that in promoting Scotland anywhere these days, one has got to concentrate on the quality image which is very rightly deserved. It's a quality experience coming to Scotland. And that is the message we've got to put over.

How effective the Saltire cross would be as a marketing tool is not entirely clear. National brands denoting country of origin are becoming increasingly important as worldwide trade barriers come down. At present, a confused message is being sent out, with the food and drink industry, the tourist trade and manufacturing firms all using variations on a number of Scottish themes. There is a need to translate the loose concept of 'Scottishness' into a strong coherent identity.

From their Strategic Development Report (May 1994), it emerges that the Scottish Tourist Board is seeking to market Scotland as a holiday destination to holiday-makers in England. In order to assist the development of appropriate marketing and advertising activity, the Board sampled responses from a cross-section of society in London, Manchester, Leeds and Birmingham.

Many of the respondents felt that, for attracting tourists to Scotland, a logo should include tartan. Most liked the Piper because they saw this as a symbol of culture and as uniquely Scottish. The Thistle was also regarded as being obviously Scottish because it was natural and colourful.

However, not all the symbols thought suitable for Scotland were appropriate as holiday logos. These included Whisky, the Stag, the Lion Rampant and the St Andrew's Cross. Other symbols, although regarded as potentially attractive, were not linked closely enough with Scotland. Among these was the Grouse, the Eagle, Mountains and Highland Cattle.

Scottish International, founded in 1995, aims to establish an alliance of the most successful Scots throughout the world, harnessing their knowledge, experience and influence for the benefit of Scotland. The organisation is not tied to any political, religious or other organisation and is non-profit making. The members of Scottish International are convinced of two things – first, that most of us in Scotland can learn from our visitors: in particular, how do we grow international companies from a Scottish base? Second, it is clear that Scots businessmen and women who have built and managed international companies in the USA, Hong Kong and elsewhere have for long sought a way of helping the country of their origins and of being interested in Scottish business affairs.

As Scottish International's prospectus comments: 'If you have a drop of Scottish blood in your veins, you have reason to be proud. The success of entrepreneurs, explorers and adventurers of Scottish descent is engraved on the history of the world.'

Participating in the inaugural meeting of Scottish International, under the chairmanship of the Earl of Airlie (among many others), were Sir Denys Henderson, Jackie Stewart OBE and Sir Adrian Swire.

Religious Significance Today

But as well as offering marketing possibilities for commerce and industry, St Andrew and the Saltire provide a window of opportunity in cultural, political and especially religious terms.

St Andrew Aid Relief (based in Edinburgh) was formed as a charitable trust in July 1994. It is committed to raising finance, collecting and transporting humanitarian aid. At the moment, the priority is Russia. 'We chose St Andrew as our patron saint,' writes co-ordinator Bob McNab, 'since he is the patron saint both of Scotland and Russia – a point appreciated by the Russians. When we visit the four schools now on our regular calling list, we find the Saltire prominently displayed.'

While the **Fellowship of St Andrew** is a Scottish group devoted to improving relations between Christians in the West and Orthodox Christians, the Convener of Action of Churches Together in Scotland (ACTS), the **Revd Maxwell Craig**, sees ecumenical possibilities in St Andrew:

> *Because Scotland is a nation – and one which has looked, for years, to Andrew as a focus of much that is best in our people, there is genuine significance in observing his day each year and giving thanks for his life.*
>
> *If you were to ask whether Andrew means more than, say, Ninian or Columba to most Scottish Christians, I would find myself on shakier ground. Andrew, as one of the first disciples, has a place in every Christian's calendar. But his link with Scotland is remote – perhaps more so than his links with Greece or with Russia, which also owe him special respect.*
>
> *I am not one of those who believe that those we call 'saints' can intercede for present-day Scots more effectively than any others in the communion of saints. I am sure there are Christian people who do rely on the intercession of the saints. For them, Andrew may be especially encouraging. As a good Presbyterian, however, my own conviction is that we have one intercessor in Jesus Christ, risen and ascended. I see no need for any other.*
>
> *Having said that, I look to a time when the Church in Scotland will become united. When that happens, a Patron Saint may have a more central role to play – and Andrew is the one to fill that role.*

The **Revd Professor Robin Barbour** takes a more sceptical view:

> *It seems to me that now the actual figure of Andrew really has no signifi-*

cance for Scotland, and even the Saltire and the diagonal cross, on which he is supposed to have been crucified, have virtually been evacuated of their original meaning. The thistle and 'wha daur meddle wi me?' probably mean more to most Scots than the death of their patron Saint, following the way of his Master, yet unwilling to be thought too like him. But I suppose that if Andrew has a potential significance for the Scots, that's where it lies.

Every now and then one hears references to Andrew as the one who brings others to Christ and Andrew as a fisherman; and I suppose that there's also a connexion in some people's minds with the importance of Andrew in the Greek Orthodox tradition. But I must say, I am a wee bit sceptical about his potential significance for us today.

Thinking about Scotland's patron saint brings the **Revd Andrew R Morton**, Assistant Director of the Centre for Theology and Public Issues, through a journey of self-discovery:

I confess to accepting without much thought the fact that Saint Andrew is the Patron Saint of Scotland, even though I bear his name.

However, I am glad that he is our Patron Saint, as he has traditionally and properly been regarded as the prototype of the missionary – his first action was to bring his brother Simon to Jesus. So he is the Patron Saint of World Mission.

The more I think about this, the more important I find it. Why? Because Scotland and its Church has an honourable record of taking the gospel to the ends of the earth; this was true of the Columban Church, of the Scottish Churches in the nineteenth and early twentieth century and at other times.

Sadly, the Church of Scotland at present is in grave danger of losing this worldwide and missionary vision and of retreating into a narrower and more self-preserving mood. We need Andrew to keep leading us out. So, yes, he is significant and should become more so.

Bishop Michael Hare Duke, the former Episcopal Bishop of St Andrews, commented:

I'm happy with the Celtic saints, their legends and their fun and games. Andrew, I feel, was a strange kind of political move. It is very difficult to take those bones from Hexham very seriously, I think. It was about getting Scotland one of the Apostles. If one wanted to have any exploration into what the name of the game was with patronage and saints in the politics of the Middle Ages — that's one thing. But an actual devotional thing, I can't feel. I can see that someone like Moluag or Fergus or Blane who thumped about the hills and had something to do with Scotland — that I can see. But to actually have imported Andrew was a bit like James of Compostela who was really all about keeping a line against the Moors.

The **Most Revd Richard F Holloway**, Bishop of Edinburgh and Primus of the Scottish Episcopal Church, said:

I am very fond of St Andrew as a character in the New Testament, especially as delineated in the three episodes in St John's gospel where he appears. He strikes me as a modest kind of man who brought people to Jesus and didn't try to push himself to the front, unlike his big brother Peter. His significance for Scotland is because he became our Patron Saint in the way of these things but it would take a very ingenious intelligence to establish a particular connection between him and Scotland other than through our meditations on the New Testament.

Archbishop Keith Patrick O'Brien, Roman Catholic Archbishop of St Andrews and Edinburgh, reflected:

If you were asked to think of one Saint who has some sort of appeal and significance to all Scots, surely that would be St Andrew.

From the earliest days of the Christian Church in Scotland, the name of this particular Saint has been associated with our country. When one thinks back to the medieval Church, then the shrine and Cathedral of St Andrew in Fife rivalled any of the great pilgrimage centres in Europe. Whilst sorrowing at the destruction of so much of our Christian heritage, particularly in St Andrews at the time of the Reformation, we still marvel at the majestic ruins of the old Cathedral in the university town.

Similarly we rejoice in the fact that relics, the visible links with St Andrew, are preserved in the St Andrew Altar in St Mary's Roman Catholic Cathedral, Edinburgh. I personally rejoice in the title of 'archbishop of St Andrews and Edinburgh' — preserving the link between the old centre of pilgrimage with the present capital.

St Andrew's Day is now more and more observed as the National Day of Scotland when all our peoples both at home and abroad, can acknowledge their one patron.

The **Revd John L Bell**, minister, musician and Liturgical Resource Worker for the Iona Community, offers a corrective opinion:

Ever since I heard the late William Barclay refer, during a St Andrew's Day sermon, to 'a dubious rickle of bones which might be buried somewhere on the East Coast', I have suspected the value of St Andrew as the Patron Saint.

Apart from the fact that he had no historically verifiable connection with Scotland, he was the least important of the inner sanctum of Christ's disciples.

It is highly anomalous that a country whose religious culture owes a great deal to Calvin should have a Patron Saint. It is part of the genius of Protestantism that we don't believe in saints – we just name our churches after them.

It it were worth the trouble, and if the Churches would wear it, I'd back either Patrick or Columba as the real Patron Saint. Patrick would probably be the first to fall, as his Irish association clouds his Scottish pedigree – that is, if he was born on the Clyde and not in Wales.

Columba would be my front-runner for a number of reasons. Firstly, like the best saints, his fallibility and eccentricities are writ large (he came to Scotland after a copyright dispute!). Secondly, he is the prime Apostle of the Celtic Church, exhibiting more of its flair and rich spirituality than either Ninian or Patrick. Thirdly, he evangelised Scotland and (lest our Southern neighbours forget), was largely responsible for the evangelisation of North and Eastern England. Fourthly, the location of his centre of mission and his burial place can be precisely located – something which cannot be said for Andrew.

From St Andrew's Scots Memorial Church in Jerusalem, the **Revd Colin Morton** offers a concluding view of St Andrew from the Holy Land:

If you stand at the Jaffa Gate or on Mount Zion and look over the Hinnom Valley, you see the Saltire flying proudly over St Andrew's Scots Memorial Church. Indeed, there are many spots in Jerusalem where St Andrew's with its flag forms part of the viewer's skyline.

Before I came to Jerusalem, I had never been responsible for flying a flag. I discovered that it was a responsibility to be taken seriously. In its very exposed position, and with desert dust, winter rain and a compass of winds, a flag does not last long. A new one soon became tattered and drab like an old regimental colour laid up in a parish church. We have to be prepared to take down the old and run up a new every six months and we are indebted to the Society of the Friends of St Andrew's whose generosity enables us to keep a supply in hand. Nevertheless, our supply has some-

times failed and there have been occasions when the white diagonals on blue could only be guessed at and even times when we have no flag at all.

Now Jerusalem is a place where it is hard to escape criticism from one quarter or another, and contrary opinions are rarely muted. But I have never experienced such fierce criticism from such a variety of sources as when we have failed to fly a decent St Andrew's flag. It has come from Scots, of course; from returning visitors and guests to St Andrew's, whatever their country, who do not like to see old traditions put at risk; from other Christians in Jerusalem who fear withdrawal of any Christian witness or presence in the Holy City; and from Jerusalemites of other faiths for whom St Andrew's, its architecture, its warmth and welcome, all that it stands for, is something precious, whose loss or diminishment would leave the city poorer and sadder.

However St Andrew came to be the patron saint of Scotland, the fact that he is means a lot here in the Holy Land. The Saltire proclaims that we are Scottish; its flying here helps keep our connection to Scotland strong, and is a joy for Scots and all who love Scotland. It is a Christian cross and proclaims our Christianity, raising fewer of the bad memories among Jews or Moslems than those aroused by some other Christian symbols. And it tells of a connection that is more important still.

Scotland is one of the few countries which have as their saint one of the disciples, and Andrew was the very first to answer Jesus' call. I do not think it is wrong to say that the Scottish Christian tradition has always looked for direct, first-hand discipleship. Scots did not see their faith filtered through other traditions or authorities, political, cultural or ecclesiastical. From early days they wished to see their own church, not under another national church. The Scottish Reformation is marked by the struggle to ensure that the Kirk is responsible directly to Christ, its only head. Its worship sought to let nothing come between the worshipper and the Word of God. Apart from its dedication to the first of Christ's disciples, St Andrew's, Jerusalem has a well-known plaque within it commemorating the wish of King Robert the Bruce that his heart should be buried in Jerusalem. The chord this strikes in so many hearts is a real one. There should be a direct connection between Scotland and the first source of its faith.

The Cross of St Andrew flies not only in Jerusalem, but at the Sea of Galilee Centre in Tiberias, where another Scottish St Andrew's Church stands beside the Sea. It also flies at Tabeetha School in Jaffa. We remember St Andrew in Galilee as the fisherman and disciple who went without a backward look to follow his Lord. We remember him in Jerusalem as a witness of the Resurrection, the Apostle of the new-found Church, and we can remember him in *Jaffa*, where he may well have set sail to carry the gospel to Greece, as the martyr who gave his life for the Master he never ceased to follow. Indeed, St Andrew makes for us a strong connection with Greece, whose patron saint he also is. The mother church in Jerusalem is the Greek Orthodox Church, tracing its unbroken descent from the Church of Pentecost. That we honour St Andrew highly, enables us better to be and be accepted as being of the one holy, universal and apostolic Church, represented with all its divisions, but more importantly in its unity, here in Jerusalem.

Scotland will never be the greatest or most prominent nation. In the Holy Land the Scottish Church is a tiny presence. I hope we can always be true followers of the man who was born in Bethlehem, taught and healed in Galilee, died and rose again in Jerusalem, whose gospel was brought to every corner of the world. I hope that we can be a blessing and support to others as Andrew was, and play our part in the feeding of the hungry and the life of the world.

St Andrew is very close and important to us in Jerusalem, no dim, distant figure. We do thank God for him and hope that Scots everywhere may always do so.

AUTHOR NIGEL TRANTER BESIDE THE SALTIRE AT ATHELSTANEFORD

BIBLIOGRAPHY

ANDERSON, M. O. (1974), *The Scottish Tradition* (Edinburgh: Scottish Academic Press).

ARNOLD-FOSTER, F. (1899), *Studies in Church Dedications of England's Patron Saints* (London: Skeffington & Son).

ASH, M. (1980), *The Strange Death of Scottish History* (Edinburgh: Ramsay Head Press).

BAIN, J., *et al*, (ed) (1881-), *Calendar of Documents relating to Scotland preserved in Her Majesty's Public Record Office* (London, Edinburgh. HM General Register House).

BARONIO, C. (1618), *Annales ecclesiastici*, vol. x [*anno* 586] (Antwerp: ex officina Plantiniana).

BAXTER, J. H. (ed) (1930), *St Andrews Copiale: Copiale Prioratus Sanctiandrew* (Oxford: Oxford University Press).

BLISS, W. H. (ed) (1893), Calendar of Entries in the Papal Registers relating to Great Britain and Ireland – *Papal Letters*, vol. 1 (London: HMSO).

BOWER, W. (1987-1991), *Scotichronicon* (Aberdeen: Aberdeen University Press).

BRADLEY, S. A. J. (trans) (1982), *Anglo-Saxon Poetry* (Everyman).

BRAUNFELS, W. (1973), *Lexikon der Christlichen Ikonographie*, vol. 5 (Vienna: Herder).

BURCH, V. (1927), *Myth and Constantine the Great* (Oxford: Oxford University Press).

BURNS, J. H (ed) (1988), 'The Scottish cult of Constantine' in *Cambridge History of Medieval Political Thought* (Cambridge: Cambridge University Press).

BURNS, C. (1976), *Calendar of Papal Letters to Scotland of Clement VII of Avignon 1378-1394* (Edinburgh: Scottish History Society).

BUTE, J. (1889), 'The last resting place of St. Andrew' in *The Scottish Review*, January 1889 (Paisley: Alex Gardner).

BUTE, J. (1894), Rectorial address delivered at the University of St Andrews (London: A. & C. Black).

BUTE, J. (1895), *The Tomb of St Andrew* (London: Alexander Gardner).

BUTLER, J. (1995), *The Quest for Becket's Bones* (New Haven, Connecticut: Yale University Press).

COLGRAVE, B. (ed) (1968), *The earliest life of Gregory the Great by an anonymous monk of Whitby* (Lawrence: University of Kansas Press).

CROSS, S. H. and SHERBOWITZ-WETZOR, O.P. (eds) (trans) (1953), *The Russian Primary Chronicle*, vol. 60 (Cambridge, Massachusetts: The Medieval Academy of America Publications).

CUTTS, E. L. (1895), *Augustine of Canterbury* (London: Methuen & Co).

DICKSON, T. et al., (ed) (1877-1978), Accounts of the Lord High Treasurer of Scotland (*Compota Thesauriariorum Regum Scotorum*) (Edinburgh: HM General Register House).

DILWORTH, M. (1974), 'The Augustinian Chaper of St Andrews' in *Innes Review*, no. 25 (Glasgow: Scottish Catholic Historical Association).

DILWORTH, M. (1994), *Whithorn Priory in the late Middle Ages* (Whithorn: Friends of the Whithorn Trust).

DONALDSON, G. and McCRAE, C. (1942-4) *St Andrews Formulare 1514-46* (Edinburgh: Stair Society).

DUDDEN, F. H. (1905), *Gregory the Great* (London: Longmans, Green and Co).

DUNCAN, T. O. (1934), *Athelstaneford* (Athelstaneford: Andrew Elliott).

DUNLOP, A. I. (1956), *Calendar of Scottish Supplications to Rome 1423-1428* (Edinburgh: Scottish History Society).

DUNLOP, A. I. and COWAN, I. B. (eds) (1970), *Calendar of Scottish Supplications to Rome 1428-1432* (Edinburgh: Scottish History Society).

DUNLOP, A. I. and MacLAUGHLAN, D. (eds) (1983), *Calendar of Scottish Supplications to Rome 1433-1447*, vol. iv (Glasgow: University of Glasgow Press).

DURKAN, J. (1962), 'Care of the Poor: Pre-Reformation Hospitals' in D. McROBERTS, *Essays* (see below).

DURKAN, J. (1974), 'St Andrews in the John Law Chronicle' in *Innes Review*, no. 25 (Glasgow: Scottish Catholic Historical Association).

DVORNIK, F. (1958), *The Idea of Apostolicity in Byzantium*, Dumbarton Oaks Studies, no. 48 (Cambridge: Harvard University Press).

FENNELL, J. (1995), *A History of the Russian Church to 1448* (London: Longman).

GILBERT, E. (1974), 'Saint Wilfrid's church at Hexham' in KIRBY (ed), *Saint Wilfrid at Hexham* (Newcastle: Oriel Press).

GLASGOW MUSEUMS (1993), *The St Mungo Museum* (Glasgow: Glasgow Museums).

GODFREY, J. (1980), *1204, The Unholy Crusade* (Oxford: Oxford University Press).

GRAGG, F. A. and GABEL, L. C. (1937-1957), Commentaries of Pius II, in the Smith College Studies in History (Northampton, Massachusetts: Smith College).

HALL, U. (1994), *St Andrew and Scotland* (St Andrews: St Andrews University Library).

HANNAY, R. K. (1934), *St Andrew of Scotland* (Edinburgh: Moray Press).

HANNAY, R. K. (ed)(trans) (1913), *Rentale Sancti Andree*, Chamberlain and Granitor Accounts of the Archbishopric in the time of Cardinal Beatoun 1538-1546 (Edinburgh: Edinburgh University Press).

HANNAY, R. K. and HAY, D. (ed) (1954), *The Letters of James V* (Edinburgh: HMSO).

HAWS, C. H. (1972), *Scottish Parish Clergy at the Reformation 1540-74* (Edinburgh: Scottish Record Society).

HAY FLEMING, D. (1889), *Register of the Ministers, Elders and Deacons of the Christian Congregation of St Andrew 1559-1600* (Edinburgh: Edinburgh University Press).

HOWORTH, H. H. (1912), *Saint Gregory the Great* (London: John Murray).

INNES, T. (1978), *Scots Heraldry* (London: Johnston & Bacon).

KAZHDAN, A. P. (ed) (1991), *The Oxford Dictionary of Byzantium*, vol. 1 (Oxford: Oxford University Press).

KEE, A. (1982), *Constantine versus Christ* (London: SCM).

LAMONT-BROWN, R. (1989), *The Life and Times of St Andrews* (Edinburgh: John Donald).

LINDSAY, E. R. and CAMERON, A. I. (1934), *Calendar of Scottish Supplications to Rome 1418-1422* (Edinburgh: Scottish History Society).

LYNCH, M. (1991), *Scotland: A New History* (London: Century).

McCRONE, D. (1992), *Understanding Scotland – The sociology of a stateless nation* (London: Routledge).

McCRONE, D., MORRIS, A. and KIELY, R. (1995), *Scotland – the Brand* (Edinburgh: Edinburgh University Press).

MacDONALD, A. A., LYNCH, M. and COWAN, I. B. (eds) (1994), *The Renaissance in Scotland: Studies in Literature, Religion, History and Culture Offered to John Durkan* (Leiden: E. J. Brill).

MacEWEN, A. (1913), *A History of the Churches in Scotland* (London: Hodder & Stoughton).

MacFARLANE, L. J. and McINTYRE, J. (eds) (1982), *Scotland and the Holy See* (Glasgow: Scottish Catholic Heritage Commission).

McGURK, F. (ed) (1976), *Calendar of Papal Letters to Scotland of Benedict XIII of Avignon 1394-1419* (Edinburgh: Scottish History Society).

McKAY, D. (1968), *The Four Heid Pilgrimages of Scotland* in *Innes Review*, no. xix (Glasgow: Scottish Catholic Historical Association).

McMILLAN, W. (1916), *Scottish Symbols* (Paisley: Alexander Gardner).

McMILLAN, W. and STEWART, J. (1925), *The Story of the Scottish Flag* (Glasgow: H. Hopkins).

McROBERTS, D. (1976), *The Glorious House of St Andrew in The Medieval Church of St Andrews* (Glasgow: Burns).

McROBERTS, D (1962), 'Material Destruction caused by the Scottish Reformation' in *Essays on the Scottish Reformation 1513-1625* (Glasgow: Burns).

MASSON, A. J. (ed) (1897), *The Mission of St Augustine to England* (Cambridge: Cambridge University Press).

PETERSON, P. M. (1958), *Andrew, Brother of Simon Peter* (Leiden: E. J. Brill).
PURSER, J. (1992), *Scotland's Music* (Edinburgh: Mainstream Publishing).
PÜTTER, J. (1994), *The Research Prints Catalogue* (St Andrews: Grafik Orzel).
QUELLER, D. E. (ed) (1971), *The Latin Conquest of Constantinople* (New York: John Wiley & Sons, Inc).
RICHARDS, J. (1980), *Consul of God* (London: Routledge & Kegan Paul).
ROSS, P. (1886), *Saint Andrew* (New York: The Scottish American).
RUBINSTEIN, R. O. (1967), Pius II's Piazza S. Pietro and St Andrew's Head in *Essays in the History of Architecture presented to Rudolf Wittkower,* (London: Phaidon Press).
SCHMIDT, S. (1992), *Augustin Bea* (New York: New City Press).
SKENE, W. F. (1860-62), 'Notice of the Early Ecclesiastical Settlements at St Andrews' in *Proceedings of the Society of Antiquaries of Scotland,* vol. iv.
SOCIETY OF ANTIQUARIES OF SCOTLAND (1855-1994), *Proceedings of Society of Antiquaries of Scotland* (Edinburgh: National Museums of Scotland).
STUART, J. and BURNETT, G., et al., (eds) (1878-1908), *The Exchequer Rolls of Scotland (Rotuli Scaccarii Regum Scotorum)* (Edinburgh: HM General Register House).
SUMPTION, J. (1975), *Pilgrimage – An Image of Medieval Religion* (London: Faber & Faber).
THOMAS, C. (1973), *Bede, Archaeology and the Cult of Relics* (Jarrow: H. Saxby).
TURNER, M. (1922), *The Life and Labour of John Menzies Strain* (Aberdeen: Aberdeen University Press).
WATT, D. E. R. (1969), *Fasti Eccelsiae Scoticane Medii Aevi* (St Andrews: Scottish Record Society).
WILSON, S. (1983), 'Saints and their Cults' in *Studies in Religious Sociology, Folklore and History* (Cambridge: Cambridge University Press).

INDEX

PICTURE CREDITS

*The etchings and illustrations in this book
are taken from the following sources:*